CHARISMA

Mark Todd

Threshold Books

First published in Great Britain by
Threshold Books
The Kenilworth Press Limited
661 Fulham Road
London SW6 5PZ

British Library Cataloguing in Publication Data
Todd, Mark
    Charisma.
    1. Eventing horses. Three-day. Charisma
    I. Title
    798.2'4

    ISBN 0-901366-78-1

Compiled by Gillian Newsum

Designed by Eddie Poulton

Typeset by Servis Filmsetting Ltd., Manchester
Colour Separation by Reed Reprographics, Ipswich
Printed and bound in England by Westway Offset

CONTENTS

ACKNOWLEDGEMENTS

Before thanking all those who have been directly involved with this book, I would like to record my gratitude to my first sponsor, Bill Hall of Woolrest International, without whose generosity and faith my partnership with Charisma would never have left the ground.

Gillian Newsum deserves special acknowledgement for the professional way in which she has brought together the story of Charisma's life.

I am particularly indebted to those who helped fill in the details of Charisma's early days in New Zealand, namely Peter and Daphne Williams, David Goodin, David Murdoch, Sharon Dearden and Jennifer Stobart; and I am grateful to Pam Bailey for organising the photo of Charisma in his retirement.

Thanks are due to Joan Gilchrist, editor of *New Zealand Horse and Pony*, for her chapter charting Charisma's career and for providing valuable information and photographs, thus filling in the missing links in his background.

Helen Gilbert merits a big thank-you, not only for her hard work and support in the years during which she worked as Charisma's groom, but also for contributing the chapter, 'The Best Horse in the World'.

I am grateful to all the riders, friends and officials who have provided the quotes which appear throughout the pages of this book; to Linda Warren who helped in the initial stages of production; to Eddie Poulton, the designer, for his skilful handling of the contents; and to Lizzie Purbrick for allowing me to tell the story of her intervention in Charisma's sale.

Finally, I would like to thank Barbara Cooper of Threshold whose idea it was to publish the book.

INTRODUCTION

Good horses come and go but I have been lucky enough to
have one who can truly be called a champion – Charisma –
and they only come along once in a lifetime. It wasn't only
his superb ability – his athleticism and lightness of stride –
that made him so good. He had something extra that
separates the good ones from the really good ones – star
quality. He had such an infectious enthusiasm for life: he
loved going places and he was always interested in what was
going on. He thrived on the competition atmosphere –
showing off to the crowds, the challenge of the cross-
country. But I think that what made him a truly great event
horse was that he loved his job.

Winning the second gold medal at the Seoul Olympics was
undoubtedly the greatest moment of his career. It was a
classic performance: a brilliant dressage test followed by a
copy-book cross-country round, finishing full of running to
prove wrong all the cynics who had said that at sixteen he
was past his best. I had always felt that he deserved the
chance to defend his title and he fully justified that faith. It
was the most perfect way for him to bow out. All his friends
and admirers will remember him for what he was – a true
Champion.

Mark Todd

1 Early Days

Charisma at three weeks old, with his mother, Planet. He was a very strong foal, with tremendous hind quarters and a powerful neck and shoulder.

Charisma was born a champion, and I'm sure he knew it. He always had an indefinable quality, even as a foal, and there was never any doubt that he was something 'special'. He was a precocious youngster and, according to his breeders, Daphne and Peter Williams, 'just loved the girls', having to be separated from the fillies at an early age! He wasn't gelded until he was nearly four, and some of his 'coltish' playfulness seems to have stayed with him. The Williamses nicknamed him 'Stroppy'.

'As a baby he was absolutely unbelievable', says Mrs Williams. 'His temperament was incredible. We have four boxes for the weanlings and you have to walk through two to get to the inside one. He was in the outside one. I used to feed the foals at eight o'clock at night, and Stroppy would always be asleep. I'd walk through with the feed buckets, then come back to him. He would look up at me, get up, eat his feed and lie down again.

'He was quite unreal when he was weaned. He never put a foot wrong. When we taught him to tie up, he tied. You could see him thinking "it's rather a bore, but I suppose if I have to stand here for an hour or so, I'll have to". He was the dearest boy.'

Even at that age Charisma obviously had a fairly laid-back attitude to life: something which stayed with him when he was jet-setting around the world competing in international events. His mother, Planet, had been a successful show jumper. Daphne had originally hunted her, and the Williams' two daughters then took her show jumping, reaching Grade A. For a while she was owned by the show jumping rider Sheryl Douglas (née Marr), and became the first mare in New Zealand to jump her own height, but an injury brought her competitive career to an early end, and she was put to stud at the Williams' 3,000-acre Mamaku Station in Wairarapa, North Island.

Planet was only 15hh, out of a Thoroughbred mare, Starbourne, by Kiritea (who was one-sixteenth Percheron). She was put to the Thoroughbred stallion Tira Mink, by Faux Tirage (champion sire in 1957–58). The liaison produced a colt foal, born on 30 October 1972.

Since moving to the Mamaku Station some thirty-five years ago, the Williamses, who came to New Zealand from England in 1947, have become well known for their success in breeding competition horses by mixing other breeds with Thoroughbreds, and Tira Mink had already sired some international show jumpers and a few good event horses before Planet was sent to him. After Charisma's performance in Los Angeles the Williamses had a lot of enquiries from overseas buyers

Tira Mink, Charisma's sire, on Mamaku Station, Wairarapa, with some of his mares. Charisma's dam, Planet, is the one with her head in the bucket . . . like mother, like son?

wanting to know if there were any relatives of the hardy little Kiwi horse available. Sadly, there were none. Planet was dead by then, and although the Williamses had retained Charisma's half-sister, High Society (by Nickola), who went to Grade B jumping, she never produced a filly at stud. Her sons, Nastasi (Medium dressage, Advanced eventer, sold to the USA) and Hardcase (Grade B show jumper, sold to Canada), are her two most successful progeny.

Venus, a full sister to Charisma, is still playing international polo in England, owned by Johnnie Kidd, but she has not had any foals. (It is certainly a versatile family; at one time, John Meyer played three full or half-sisters to Charisma in his polo team.) Another sister, Lunar, had a colt by Silent Hunter, but then suffered infertility problems, and did not produce a filly. However, last year, Lunar's owners, Mr and Mrs Fred Maunsell, put the mare into an embryo transfer programme at the Denfield Farm in Wairarapa. The result was a filly foal by Laughton's Legend, an Irish Draught. Now, at last, there is hope that Charisma's bloodline will be continued.

The Williamses didn't keep Charisma for long. Before he was weaned, the little colt had been spotted – and purchased – by David Murdoch. Charisma had created quite an impression, even at that early age, as David Murdoch explains:

'Towards the end of 1972 I returned home from England, having taken my BHSI, and worked on yards there and in Europe. My plan was to set up an equestrian centre at Isola near Auckland, where my parents farmed, and soon after I got back I went down to stay with the Williamses at Mamaku Stud. I already knew Daphne and Peter

ABOVE: David Murdoch, director of the Isola Equestrian Centre, bought Charisma as a yearling colt and gave him his early education. ABOVE RIGHT: High Society, Planet's first foal and half-sister to Charisma. The family likeness is very evident.

ABOVE: Planet and Venus, a full sister to Charisma, exported to Britain as a polo pony. RIGHT: Johnnie Kidd in action with Venus.

Lunar, a full sister to Charisma. The eyes, ears and profile are very similar.

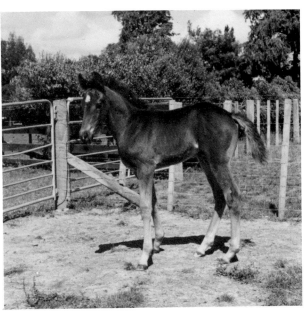

Lunar's only filly foal, by Laughton's Legend. It is hoped that she will continue the bloodline.

Charisma and Bert (Night Life) relaxing at home on our family farm in New Zealand, 1983.

well, and thought it would be a good place to start looking for horses to set up my business.

'When I arrived at the stud I could see from the driveway a black colt foal standing in the field about 300 yards from me. The moment I saw him I knew I wanted to buy him. It was his outlook that impressed me so much. He had such a bold attitude, a bright eye and an intelligent look about him, as if to say: "Watch me, I'm special." He always had that presence, in a dressage arena, show jumping or whatever. He was a real show-off.

'I told the Williamses that I wanted to buy him, and after he'd been weaned I went to fetch him. I had been down to a show near Wairarapa, and collected him on my way back, staying the night with the Meyers at Hawera. We put the yearling out for the night in a field that had a 4ft wire fence, but he obviously became bored, or hungry, and by the next morning he'd jumped out. He certainly had a lot of personality, even at that age.

'For the next couple of years he spent most of his time turned out with two other colts at David Goodin's dairy farm at Te Kauwhata, south of Auckland, and we gelded him when he was three. We took our time breaking him in – establishing everything slowly and building up his trust, but he was never any problem. Everything we did with him was really easy. He was very quick to learn, very willing and very smart, and even in those early stages was always a really nice, uncomplicated horse to ride. He had a calm, confident approach to everything, and he had a wonderful jump. Within six months of

The Isola Equestrian Centre, located south of Auckland city. It was here that Charisma's talent for jumping was first discovered.

leaving us, as a four-year-old rising five, he was competing at Grade B show jumping. My only disappointment was that he didn't grow bigger.

'I always thought that he was a special horse, but business is business and when Sharon Dearden, a pupil at our equestrian centre, wanted to buy him I had to let him go, particularly as the price she paid was exceptionally high at that time – about NZ$3,500 (£1300). Sharon was a good rider on ponies, but Charisma was her first horse and with him she had tremendous success.'

Sharon Dearden and Charisma competing in the New Zealand Pony Club Championships at Ashburton in 1981. A shy after the final fence in the show-jumping phase caused them to miss the finish flags, dropping them into second place.

Sharon Dearden takes up the story:

'My time with Charisma, or "Stroppy" as he was known then, began at the end of August 1977. After competing at the 1977 New Zealand Pony Club Championships with my pony Royal Tudor, I found myself, at the age of fourteen, too tall to ride ponies any longer. In an attempt to find a new hack I went from my home at Christchurch to the Isola Equestrian Centre in Auckland to be a working pupil and to look at some horses for sale there.

'On initial inspection I was drawn to a skewbald colt; Stroppy was merely "the black gelding". But after several rides and lessons with David Murdoch I began to realise the potential of the black gelding. David had bought Stroppy as a prospective show jumper, but on realising that he was destined to be forever "the *little* black gelding", he decided to offer him to me. In those days Stroppy was a typical young horse with immense determination and will power. As he was extremely proud and always keen to be noticed, he acquired the name "Charisma".

'He was sent to Christchurch in November 1977, and we picked him up and drove the fifty miles to our property. He quickly settled into his new surroundings, but just as quickly showed that he was not going to be "easy". He was still rather colty and was forever tossing things around his paddock. During the Christmas school holidays I went back to Isola as a working pupil, but was soon summoned home again after Charisma began chasing everyone out of his paddock and became extremely difficult to handle.

'I think now of these months as our "testing" time. Most of it was spent having arguments about absolutely everything: which way to go, what speed to go, and when to stop! Living in a farming community meant that there were plenty of opportunities for riding, including doing the lambing beat and mustering. With this consistent and varied work he quickly began to realise that it wasn't so bad after all. He learnt to cross rivers, carry sheep, jump fences and gates almost anywhere and go into very steep country. In those days Badminton and the Olympics were things to be watched and admired from afar, and not for one moment did anyone think that all those places he jumped into and out of and went through and around would ever stand him in good stead for his later achievements.

'Slowly but surely he began to settle down and to show some of his potential. On his very first outing – just a few show classes at a local show – he won his Maiden Hack class, and when presented with his ribbon proceeded to dispose of me and gallop around the centre ring to show off!

'However, things looked to be improving, and we started competing at Pony Club events and some Horse Society days. Just when things started to go right and he was competing at Novice FEI show jumping and dressage events, things suddenly went really wrong. For no apparent reason he began refusing to turn right. For two or three months I persevered with everything I knew, to try to solve this problem, and was continually frustrated when we were eliminated many times for not being able to get through the start flags or for getting stuck half-way round a course or during a test with a right-handed turn. In those days there were many tears and many arguments, but eventually under the ever-watchful eye of our National Trainer, Lockie Richards, and a return to basic ground work, we finally overcame the problem.

'By August 1979 Charisma had become a Novice Dressage Champion, a Champion Show Hack, a Champion Paced and Mannered Hack, and Champion Hunter; and had won for me the Junior Equitation Finals. In May 1979 we were in the Canterbury Westland Area Team to go to the New Zealand Pony Club Championships at Wanganui, where our team came fourth, and later that year we were selected for the South Island Horse Society Dressage Team and were upgraded to Grade C show jumping.

'In 1980 I became a student at Christchurch Teachers' Training College, and during the beginning of the year boarded with Sue Alleyne from Christchurch, who was then riding Johann Strauss, a Medium dressage horse. Under her constant guidance, and with more careful instruction from Lockie, we upgraded to Medium.

'During that year we continued to compete at Pony Club events, at which Charisma was rarely out of first place. We also competed in Horse Society dressage and show jumping competitions, and in horse trials. We gained many places in Medium and Prix St George dressage classes and were upgraded to Grade B show jumping.

'In May we again went with the Canterbury Westland team to the New Zealand Pony Club Championships at Masterton, where we won the D.C. Dressage Cup – but, unfortunately, with a run-out at a corner on the cross-country we missed out on an overall placing. During the show jumping phase he over-reached badly, and after being stitched and put in plaster we missed our chance at our very first three-day event.

'1981 was perhaps the most successful year we had together, and it was extremely rewarding. His dressage continued to progress and he was rarely unplaced in competition. That year, as I was now seventeen, we rode in the A1 (17–21) section of the NZPC Championships at Ashburton, where we won the A1 Dressage Cup and were still in the lead going in to the show jumping. This was extremely exciting, as we were on home territory and the crowd especially wanted someone from the area to win. After we jumped the final fence clear, the crowd rose clapping and cheering – causing us to shy and miss the flags! Unfortunately, this fault was enough to drop us into second place overall.

'Two weeks later at the National Novice Three-Day Event we made no such mistake, and won, still on our dressage score of 6.7.

'In 1982 things carried on in much the same way. We began the year by winning the Canterbury One-Day Event, on the strength of which we again gained a place with the Canterbury Westland team to compete in the NZPC Championships, this time in Auckland. Two weeks before we were due to leave, we were riding at a training session at the racecourse. After jumping a relatively easy fence, Charisma stumbled, and I landed on my shoulder breaking my collarbone. As there was no reserve that year, I went to Auckland with the team. We again led in the dressage, and then had to face a course that was probably the most controversial in the history of NZPC Championships. Things went astray for us at Fence 2, which was a drop parallel. Having landed with a great deal of force on my right arm, I was unable to use it for the rest of the way around. Dear Charisma just carried on (at a somewhat lesser pace) and nursed us home, with a cricket score of time faults – but safe. Not long afterwards, in June, we went on to win the Canterbury Intermediate Two-Day Event.

'After returning home and back to Training College I was faced with some major decisions about area placement for my Year One teaching position. Around this time Charisma and I were also put on the short list for Los Angeles, but for many personal reasons – added to the fact that I was required to do my Year One teaching immediately upon finishing my training – I decided that the best thing to do was to sell Charisma.

'Naturally I had had many large offers for him, but I had always turned them down, wanting to find the right home rather than the right price. Eventually I was approached by Mrs Fran Clark of Taupo who wanted the horse for herself, and whose children could continue with him later. This sort of "family" home was what I was seeking for my best friend.

'As I had received a Year One teaching position at Mt Maunganui, I travelled with the horse to Taupo, only a two-hour drive away. I stayed with Charisma for a week and then left him in Taupo. Fortunately, my association with him didn't end there, and when Mark took him over, Fran made an effort to keep me involved.

'It wasn't an easy time, and several disagreeable things happened which could not have been foreseen. However, Fran – well aware of Charisma's ability and knowing that it needed to be nurtured – eventually asked Jennifer Stobart to take him in hand.

'People say you only ever get one special horse and I guess I've had mine. Charisma has always had an extremely lively personality, has loved to show off and has loved people. He was not always easy, but he was always fun. The people of Canterbury still regard him as theirs, and we are all extremely proud of both him and Mark.'

From Jennifer Stobart

'In 1981, when I first met Charisma, I was based at the National Equestrian Centre at Taupo, having taken over the post of Instructor there from Lockie Richards. Sharon and Charisma turned up on a North Canterbury course held at Claxby, where I was training competitors for the Pony Club Championships to be held later that month in Ashburton. Charisma was already known in Canterbury as a very impressive all-rounder. Lockie had been his most regular trainer, especially for dressage, for which he was graded Medium. He had been a champion hack many times and had seldom been beaten in "Round the Ring" hunter classes (a rapid, New Zealand version of working hunters). Sharon and he had hunted for two seasons with the Christchurch Hunt, and he had somehow managed to become a Grade B show jumper. He had already been twice to the Pony Club Championships in North Island, winning the dressage section the previous year at Masterton.

'The first time I rode Charisma was in 1982, when Sharon had broken her collarbone, and I was helping her out with his training. He was a great feeling to ride, with a strong, supple back and quite a deep body to take up my long legs. After the championships that year

Jennifer Stobart riding Charisma in a demonstration for Pony Club riders in New Zealand, 1982.

'NO, not all in one go!' Charisma takes me through the quick route at the 'Flying Nun', a big bank with a ditch before and wide ramp off. Benson and Hedges Three-Day Event, Taupo, 1983.

Sharon told me that she would have to sell him. As I was going to England I took some pictures of him with me, to try and interest people whom I met at horse trials, but no one felt inclined to gamble on a rather small, unknown horse on the other side of the world. When I got back to the Equestrian Centre I found to my surprise that Charisma had been bought by Mrs Fran Clark, who lived in Taupo.

'Charisma came to the Equestrian Centre to be ridden by one of our working pupils while Fran was moving house and setting up her new stables, and later on Fran asked me to ride him at the Horse of the Year. I found him an exhilarating ride, and worked him up to Prix St George standard. Just for fun, one day I popped him over some of our show jumps – he felt like a rocket taking off! He ended up in fourth place in Medium 37 for Dressage Horse of the Year.

'In May that year Mark came to look at him, and I think he was a bit taken aback to see the overgrown pony in his thick woolly coat. Fortunately, he still decided to take him on, and the rest is history. A month later at our own three-day trials I was escorting the TV crew around. Charisma was approaching the short route at the "Flying Nun" – a big bank with a ditch before and a wide ramp off – and Mark was heard to say: "NO, not all in one go!" Charisma's legs duly touched down, for an instant, on top, and I knew then that the horse was in the best of hands.'

2 Our Partnership Begins

The first time I saw Charisma was in 1975. I was working for David Goodin, another keen event rider, on his dairy farm at Te Kauwhata. I remember noticing a little black horse out on the hills, and thinking that he was quite nice but very small. That was Charisma. He was then a precocious three-year-old colt who had been sent over to graze at David Goodin's place by his owner, David Murdoch. There was another horse with him called Carlsberg (now Night Life), who I later discovered was Charisma's half-brother (they were both by Tira Mink), and who, in 1984, travelled to England with Charisma to compete at Badminton.

At that time I was riding a big, rangy chestnut called Top Hunter whom I'd bought from Lyall Keyte. He'd been going well for me at events in New Zealand and in 1978 I took him to my first international event – the World Championships in Lexington, Kentucky. The heat and humidity there made it one of the toughest championships I've ever competed in, and, along with many others, I had to retire from the cross-country. Top Hunter had injured a tendon, and couldn't go on.

Three years later I came across Charisma again, at the Pony Club Championships. I was there as trainer for my local team, and Sharon Dearden, from the Canterbury Westland branch, was riding the horse that everyone had been raving about. I had no idea it was the same horse that I'd seen at David Goodin's, and all I remember about him from the Pony Club event was that, although he did look a nice type, he was incredibly fat. I didn't give him another thought until one day in 1983 I was asked, out of the blue, if I'd like to event him.

I was in England at the time. Mimi May had asked me to ride Felix Too at Badminton because Angela Tucker, who had been competing with him, had injured herself. I had met Mimi and her husband, Tom, at a party when I had been in England competing with Southern Comfort (my Badminton winner in 1980). Mimi had asked me if I'd mind schooling Felix Too for her. I liked the horse very much, and did some competitions with him, progressing from Novice to Advanced in just one year. However, at the end of that season I decided to return home because I didn't have a suitable horse for the 1982 World Championships and there didn't seem much point in staying in England.

After my ride on Felix Too at Badminton, where we finished ninth, I had a phone call from Virginia Caro, the publicity officer for the New Zealand Horse Society. Virginia knew that I didn't have a good horse to ride at the three-day event at home in June, and she said that she had found one who might be suitable. Would I be interested? By then Charisma had been sold to Fran Clark, and was being ridden in Medium

ABOVE: Sharon Dearden and Charisma end up as reserve champions on their first time out, at Kirwee Show in 1978. RIGHT: Sharon and Charisma in the New Zealand Pony Club Championships in Auckland, 1982. BELOW: A very podgy Charisma flying the Footbridge on our way to winning the New Zealand National One-Day Championships, 1983.

ABOVE: Back at Isola, show jumping in 1983. Podge showing that he could pick up his knees when he wanted to.
RIGHT: Podge and me, proud winners of the Advanced Championship in the National Three-Day Event, 1983. Podge was clipped out except for his head, which shows how woolly he could become in the winter.

level dressage competitions by Jennifer Stobart. I agreed, tentatively, to the idea, but said that they would have to wait until I got home and saw the horse before I could make up my mind.

I knew that Charisma had a good track record. He had done well in Pony Club events and Novice horse trials, he had show jumped to Grade B level, and he was a Medium dressage horse; but when I saw him at Fran Clark's home at Taupo I very nearly got straight back in my car and drove home again. It was the beginning of winter in New Zealand. I had driven two hours to see the horse, and when I arrived they produced this very fat, hairy little creature who didn't look as if he could possibly be a suitable event horse for me. He was only 15.3hh, and I am 6ft 4in.

Having gone all that way to see him, I thought I might as well just sit on him. The first thing that struck me was that he didn't ride like a small horse. Normally my long legs hang down too far on anything small or narrow, and then I can't get my leg on the horse, but Charisma had tremendous depth of girth. He also had a very good length of rein, and terrific movement. He did feel a bit strange at the trot, though, because – despite having a big stride – he trotted with a sort of rolling motion. Even when he eventually lost weight he still used to roll, and whenever I got on him after a long break, the movement always struck me as odd.

I rode him around for a while, and he seemed to jump quite well, so I decided that although he was unlikely to make an international eventer he would be quite a good horse to ride in the one-day events that year. I already had three other horses at home, and only six weeks in which to prepare them all for the National Championship. None of them was fit, so I had a lot of work to do.

I entered Charisma and the others for a couple of one-day events before the National competition. Charisma won them both, which was encouraging. He then won the National One-Day Event Championship, followed by the National Three-Day Event – his fourth consecutive victory. Obviously his dressage training helped a great deal, and I found I was getting better marks than I had ever achieved before, but he was also proving an excellent cross-country horse. Each time I rode him he felt better and better, and I got to like him more and more.

Although he had done a good deal of dressage, he didn't go exactly as I would have liked him to, and initially I had a few lessons from the German trainer Christian Theiss, who was the official three-day event dressage coach in New Zealand. Once in England, I took lessons from Bill Noble. Throughout his career Charisma was never an easy horse to ride in dressage. Although he had tremendous natural ability – he was well-balanced, very powerful and a good mover – he was also very strong-willed. He couldn't be forced into anything, and I often found it difficult to keep him round and active.

His jumping also needed a bit of work. Sharon Dearden had warned me that he liked to slow down in front of cross-country fences and take a good look, but I found that after a bit of firm riding he soon began going more freely. His show jumping wasn't the greatest. Even though he'd got to Grade B, he was always a bit dodgy because he seemed to like to 'feel' his way round the jumps, tapping them with his feet. He had tremendous scope, but wasn't very careful.

As he had achieved such good results in his first four events with me, the New Zealand Horse Society asked if he would be available for the Olympic Games in Los Angeles the following year. I talked to Fran Clark about it, and she agreed that the horse could go, but pointed out that he wasn't for sale. I had to try and find some financial backing for the trip, as I'd decided that the best preparation for the horse would be to take him to England at the beginning of 1984 to compete at Badminton.

At that time I was looking after my own dairy herd on my grandfather's farm near Cambridge, North Island, and I often gave riding lessons to raise some extra money. On Wednesday afternoons I taught a group of three ladies, and one of them, Shirley Downey, knew Bill Hall. Apparently his company, Woolrest International, had looked into sponsoring a marathon in New Zealand but the deal had fallen through. Shirley offered to contact Bill to see if he might be interested in sponsoring me. The following day Bill rang me and arranged a meeting within a couple of days. At the meeting I told him what I wanted to do, what I needed, and how much it would all cost. The next day he rang me to say he'd do it. It all happened so quickly, but that's the sort of man Bill is: if he likes an idea he just gets on with it. As it turned out, his wife Judy was very interested in horses (she is now doing some eventing). It was just one of those lucky things. I got on really well with them both, and we became great friends.

Fran Clark wouldn't sell Charisma to Woolrest, but she eventually agreed to lease him and to let him compete under the company's name. I then arranged to rent some stables in England from Charlie Cottenham, with a cottage for me to live in. Although Woolrest were paying for the shipping of my horses to England, and for their keep over there, I realised that I was going to have to sell my dairy herd. There was no one else to look after the cows, and if I was going to be away for the best part of the year I couldn't hope to keep them. It was a difficult decision, because the herd was my livelihood, and I was taking quite a risk in giving that up to compete in the Olympic Games. If I didn't get to Los Angeles, it would all be for nothing.

By now Helen Gilbert had arrived from England to take over the job of looking after my horses, and things were becoming well organised. Charisma – nicknamed 'Podge' because of his figure – was put on a strict diet, but it was always difficult to slim him down. He was just like one of those fat children's ponies who seem to live off the smell of food, and even when he was put on half rations he did too well for himself.

In December 1983 he had competed in, and won, the New Zealand Olympic Trial – a one-day event organised specially for the long-listed riders. It was the first time that New Zealand had sent a team to the Olympics, and because we didn't have an internationally rated event this one had to be approved by the FEI. So the chairman of the FEI Three-Day Event Committee, Vicomte Jurien de la Gravière, came over to watch the event, and presented certificates of capability to all those who had jumped the cross-country well. It was a reasonably big course for a one-day event, but not as difficult as most of the advanced courses in England, so Podge would be taking a big step up when he went to compete there in the following spring, especially if he was going to run at Badminton.

I didn't have any qualms about his ability to do it. Although he had never tackled anything as big as Badminton, he had already jumped a lot of fences and gained a lot of experience. It wouldn't be like taking a novice horse. Podge was eleven years old, he had competed in plenty of events, and he was confident in himself. He was certainly ready to try something bigger, and I was happy enough that he wasn't being put out

Vicomte Jurien de la Gravière (FEI judge, France):

'In December 1983 I was asked to go to New Zealand to watch the Olympic Qualifying Horse Trials at Taupo, and to give Certificates of Capability to the horses competing there. I was quite impressed by the going – good volcanic ground – and the quality of horses and riders. Eighteen horses had been selected for the trials, among them Just Henry, Jade and Charisma. I still have the notes that I made on December 18th, 1983:

'"Charisma: Petit cheval – très, très bon equilibra. Peut progressé en dressage. Cavalier super."

'I am glad and proud to have met that marvellous horse before he came to Europe.'

ABOVE: Charisma, full of running at the last fence in the National Three-Day Event, Taupo, 1983. LEFT: Trotting up, Kiwi style, at Taupo.

ABOVE: Fran Clark, then Charisma's owner, joins us for a victory photograph after the National Three-Day Event, 1983. RIGHT: Charisma in a good outline before entering the arena for his test in the dressage phase of the National Three-Day Event in 1983. Throughout his career he was never an easy horse to ride in dressage, yet he had fantastic natural ability.

of his depth or being asked something he wasn't capable of doing. He was more experienced than Southern Comfort had been when he won Badminton in 1980.

Podge travelled to England with his half-brother Carlsberg, who had now been renamed 'Night Life'. Both horses were entered for Badminton, but on the flight over, Night Life developed some sort of travel virus, and was quite sick when he arrived. It took him a while to recover, and because I couldn't do any work with him for a couple of weeks I decided I'd have to withdraw him from Badminton. Podge, on the other hand, travelled really well. He had such a laid-back attitude to life that nothing ever seemed to bother him, and as long as he had some food to get his teeth into he was quite happy. The only problem was that he contracted an infection in his sinuses which caused a discharge from his nose. I was a bit concerned about this to start with, but it didn't seem to affect his work.

I arrived at our first event in England full of confidence. I had brought over this new horse, who'd been unbeaten in his last five outings, and was expecting to do quite well. Although the standard in New Zealand wasn't that high, I knew from having competed in England in the past that Podge was up to footing it with the best over here. Our first one-day event was Aldon, and everything went well to start with. We finished second to Lucinda Green and Regal Realm in the dressage and went clear in the show jumping, but then we had a run-out on the cross-country. It was the first time Podge had done that – I think I must have misjudged my line – and I felt a bit deflated. We hadn't made a very good start.

The next event, Rushall, was even worse: we had a fall at the last fence on the cross-country. The ground was muddy and wet, which I later learned was Podge's least favourite going, and he slipped as he took off over the first part of the fence, catching his knees on the rails and flipping me over his head.

This wasn't doing much for his confidence, or mine. There were only two weeks to go before Badminton, and we hadn't got round an event without faults. I decided to take him to Brigstock, which was only three days after Rushall, but I knew we were both in need of a successful outing. If he didn't go well there I wasn't going to start him at Badminton.

The Open Intermediate course at Brigstock was big and the ground was still quite heavy, so I took Podge slowly, just aiming to ride round without any problems. He went all right, and although he slipped a bit at the last fence, he managed to stay on his feet and crawl over. It was a great relief. Now I felt a little happier about taking him to Badminton.

Despite our somewhat discouraging performances since arriving in England, Colonel Frank Weldon, Badminton's director, seemed to have even more confidence in Charisma than I did. He wrote the following comments in his Badminton preview in *Horse and Hound*: 'It would not surprise me to see Mark Todd win the Whitbread Trophy again – for Charisma, unbeaten in his five outings at home last season, is infinitely

Podge, keen and enjoying his cross-country round at his second one-day event in England, at Rushall in 1984. His keenness led to his downfall at the next fence, where he caught his knees on the rails and flipped me over his head.

more experienced than Southern Comfort was when he came to Badminton four years ago.' As it turned out, he was almost right.

Podge was brilliant at Badminton. He wasn't at all upset by the crowds – the biggest he'd ever seen in his life. He thought they were there for him, and he loved it. He jumped round the cross-country course like a stag, finishing inside the time, and then went clear in the show jumping. If our dressage had been better, we might even have beaten Lucinda Green (on Beagle Bay) who clocked up an incredible sixth win at Badminton that year.

In the early stages, Podge wasn't easy to ride in a dressage test, especially in his transitions. He would get tense and tight, his head would come up, and it was difficult to keep him going forward into the hands. At Badminton he had been going quite well in the practice area, but once we were inside the arena I couldn't keep him totally attentive to me, and he broke a couple of times in the medium trot circles. Because he had such tremendous presence and paces he was given quite good marks, but I knew there were little things that could be improved on to achieve a really good test. Nevertheless, our score of 57.4 put us into sixth place, only six points behind Lucinda, who went straight into the lead at that stage.

As it was an Olympic year, the cross-country course wasn't quite as long as usual, and I don't think it was such a difficult course as the one I'd ridden on Southern Comfort. The track ran in an anti-clockwise direction, and the first serious question came at Fence 4, the Cattle Crush, which offered a number of alternatives. I chose a route down the left hand side – a big parallel in and two short strides to a parallel out. I had to throttle him back for that, but he jumped it quiet well. The next few fences were no problem; we jumped the corner of the Vicarage Vee, and went through the middle of the Dumb-bell.

At the Lake I had originally planned to take the shortest possible route over the log pile on the right hand side, into the water, and then turn sharp right to come out over the bank and rail. But Podge took such a big leap into the water that it was immediately evident we wouldn't make the turn, so we went on through the lake to come out over a brush fence on the left hand side. It was a longer route, but I don't think we wasted much time.

I also decided to take the long route at the Pig Sty. I had watched some of the earlier riders go through the direct way, including Lucinda on Village Gossip, and it had seemed to be a bit of a struggle for them, so I thought I'd better play it safe, which is what most of the other riders did. Podge then jumped the Keeper's Rails and the Quarry so well that I was tempted to go through the middle of the Catherine Wheel, but again decided that it was too much of a risk at that stage of the course, so we went down the left hand side.

Podge had kept up a good gallop all the way. He hadn't found it an effort, and there hadn't been any fences which had caused him problems. At Horsens Bridge we had met the fence on a bit of a long stride, so I just gave him a crack of the stick on take-off, and that really set him alight. As soon as he landed, he was off, as if to say: 'If you want me to go, I'll go!' He was a horse that needed steadying back most of the time rather than pushing. I rarely had to use my stick. If I did, it was usually just as a reminder to keep his mind on the job, and it was often more for my benefit than his.

It didn't surprise me that Podge had tackled the course so well,

> **Bill Hall *(Director of Woolrest International)*:**
>
> 'When I offered to sponsor Mark in 1983 my company, Woolrest, was doing well and I thought it would be fun to get involved in eventing because my wife, Judy, competed at novice level.
>
> 'The first meeting was with a very shy farmer who found it difficult to express his needs. The rest is history: two gold medals and a hell of a lot of fun. There was also the occasional disappointment. I shall never forget Charisma knocking down the last show jump at Badminton in 1985 – I was all dressed up to meet the Queen!
>
> 'Mark says he would never have made the big time without my support, but in return Woolrest and my profile were greatly enhanced as a result of becoming involved with Mark. I am proud to own Charisma – a national hero. He and Mark have done so much not just for New Zealand eventing but also for our national pride.'

though I think his supporters – Fran Clark and Bill and Judy Hall – who'd come over to England to watch him, were quite taken back. We'd certainly made some mistakes earlier in the season, but most of them had been silly ones, and I knew that if we could just get our act together at Badminton we would be all right. Even so, I was delighted with his performance. He'd never once felt out of his depth. A lot of people at home had said that it would be no good taking a small horse round a course like Badminton, but he had such tremendous scope that the size of fences never bothered him. Later on, when he became more confident, he would often take off much too early in front of a fence, but would still land well out the other side of it.

Podge's good cross-country put us into second place behind Lucinda, who could afford to have a fence down in the show jumping, but she didn't even need that, and jumped a clear round to hold on to her lead. It would have been nice for Podge to have won, but I wasn't disappointed. There would be other occasions, and at least I could feel confident in his ability to cope with an Olympic course. Little did I know then that he would never win a three-day event in England.

Podge had a bit of a break, and soon became fat again. I was still worried about his nasal discharge, which had been quite bad at Badminton, so when he came up to work we had his nose X-rayed. The X-ray showed a lot of fluid in his sinuses, and he was put on a dose of penicillin. The treatment seemed to work, and the discharge dried up for a while, but it was a problem that we never managed to completely cure. Throughout his career he always had a slight discharge, though it was never as bad again as it had been at that first Badminton, and it never seemed to affect his work. Later on, we used to give him garlic and inhalations to help keep his nasal passages clear, as it was always something that we were a little bit wary of.

In preparation for Los Angeles I took Podge to Tweseldown, where we finished fourth, and then to Castle Ashby where the British riders were having their final selection trial. The New Zealand team had already been announced: Charisma and me (with Night Life as my reserve horse), Mary Hamilton with Whist, and Andrew Nicholson with Kahlua, who had both gone clear at Badminton, and Andrew Bennie with Jade who had done well at the three-day event in New Zealand.

> **Geoffrey Lane (Department of Veterinary Surgery, Bristol University):**
>
> 'I first encountered Charisma in the spring of 1984, when he was afflicted with what seemed to be a straightforward sinus infection. This responded well to medical treatment, but in October 1987 the horse came back to me because the left sided nasal discharge had increased. At no time did the patient show any evidence of pain in the region of the paranasal sinuses, and, at worst, the presence of the discharge caused him to flick his head through irritation.
>
> 'The examination of October 1987 confirmed that there was considerable change within the nasal pasages and a general ongoing low level of infection. At no time did Charisma have surgery for the sinus disorder, although I have no doubt that it will be with him for the rest of his days. In conclusion, although this horse has been afflicted with a bizarre destructive infection within the nasal chambers and sinuses for several years, it does not appear to have caused him any pain and certainly has not interfered with his performance.'

At Castle Ashby Podge was very full of himself. He had no problems on the cross-country, and we finished third to Ian Stark and Ginny Holgate (now Leng). As this was our last outing before Los Angeles, it was a great boost to me that everything had gone well. The only hiccup in our preparations happened a week before we were due to leave, when Helen found a swelling on one of Podge's back legs. It caused a bit of a panic, but Wally Niederer, our team vet, who arrived in England a few days later, was confident that it was just a bump. Podge wasn't lame, and, much to my relief, the swelling soon went down. Now there was nothing to stop us going to the Olympics.

Podge being very neat and careful at the Catherine Wheel, near the end of the course at Badminton, 1984. Note the white discharge from his nose – caused by the sinus condition which stayed with him until the end of his career but which never affected his performance.

LEFT: The early stages of the warm-up for the dressage, Badminton, 1984.

BELOW: A lovely study of Charisma, clearing a fence in his faultless show-jumping round at Badminton, 1984, where we were second to Lucinda Green and Beagle Bay.

LEFT: The New Zealand team lining up for the parade before the show jumping at the Los Angeles Olympics, 1984. From left to right: Charisma and me, Andrew Bennie and Jade, Mary Hamilton (now Darby) and Whist, and Andrew Nicholson and Kahlua.

BELOW: Walking round one of the lovely tree-lined areas at Santa Anita Racecourse, preparing for the vets' inspection. My height, as usual, diminishes his!

Charisma showing his tremendous power and elegance in an extended trot in the dressage phase.

3 The First Olympic Victory

Los Angeles was really hot, with temperatures often in the 90s, and at times the smog was so thick that it became oppressive. Yet the conditions obviously suited Podge, who settled in really well. He seemed to thrive in the heat and to enjoy working on the hard ground. He'd had a terrible journey out there: his plane had been delayed twice, once at Stansted airport and then again on arrival at Los Angeles, but he'd recovered from it all remarkably quickly.

The New Zealand horses had flown out with the British and Irish teams on 18 July, ten days before the first dressage tests began. They had joined a DC8 that had come from Italy with the Italian and French horses already on board. Helen was travelling with Podge, and I went on a separate flight from Gatwick with the other riders. Apparently, as the DC8 landed at Stansted it burst a tyre. The accident was blamed on freight which had been loaded unevenly in Italy: so while our horses, plus those of the British and Irish teams, were loaded on to the plane, all the French and Italian freight was taken off. It then had to be weighed and re-loaded before our own freight could be put on. The operation was a lengthy one, and it took about five hours before the 37 horses on board the plane could begin their 13-hour flight to Los Angeles.

They arrived at 1 o'clock the next morning (local time) only to be confronted with more delays. I had gone to the airport to meet them, and was amazed at how long it took to get everything sorted out. Some of the horses were still on the 'plane two and a half hours after it arrived.

To start with, it took the American handling staff half an hour just to get the ramp in position, and then the authorities insisted that each horse had its feet picked out and scrubbed before walking on to the tarmac. By the time all the horses had been blood-tested, the grooms and other passengers accredited, and the horses loaded up and boxed for the hour's journey to Santa Anita racecourse – site of the Equestrian Games – it was 5am.

The horses were bedded down in the quarantine area, and we then had to find our way to our lodgings in the Olympic village at the University of California, another hour's drive away, before we could collapse into bed. It was a pity that we couldn't have been nearer the horses, but there was nothing we could do about the arrangements. The New Zealand team's finances weren't exactly flush – I'd had enough trouble just persuading our Horse Society that we needed more than two grooms for four horses – so we were hardly in a position to ask for more money to pay for separate accommodation near the horses. Unlike the British, who raise a great deal of money through the Horse Trials

Support Group, in New Zealand there just isn't the same the interest in the sport.

After 36 hours in the quarantine block, our horses were moved into their permanent stables. Podge had already fully recovered from the flight. Most horses lose a bit of condition after a long flight, but not him. If anything, he put on condition because he drank and ate all the way. He seemed to thrive on it all out there; he was very fit and he looked tremendous. Bill Noble, who'd been training me in England, came out as the team's dressage trainer, which was a great help, and every day Podge seemed to go better. He was relaxed and working well. He loved the routine and the constant attention of being at a big three-day event.

We used to catch the 5.30am shuttle bus from our accommodation at the University out to Santa Anita, and ride the horses in the early morning. The training facilities at the racecourse were excellent. There were plenty of practice arenas, which we shared in strict rotation with the other competitors, and for faster work we could use the turf track with its four furlong uphill 'tail'. I didn't do much jumping with Podge, because he always went better if he was fresh to it – especially in the show jumping. The more you did with him, the more blasé he became about it.

The competition area was set out on the 'home stretch' of the racecourse in front of the main grandstand, and temporary stands enclosed its three remaining sides. On dressage days these were packed almost to capacity, with a noisy, volatile crowd. I think the trouble was that the majority of the spectators had little idea of what the dressage test was all about: so instead of the respectable hush that descends on the crowd at, say, Badminton, where people hardly dare move until a test is over, in Los Angeles we were greeted with claps and cheers every time that something 'exciting' happened.

Charisma loves performing for a crowd. He's a natural showman and a great poseur. I think the atmosphere suited him, but he did lose a bit of concentration. Unfortunately, when we were warming up in the stadium around the edge of the dressage arena just before we were

---

Mary Darby (née Hamilton, New Zealand Olympic team competitor, 1988):

'At Los Angeles, before the start of the three-day event competition, I was talking to Tad Coffin (gold medal winner at the Montreal Olympics on Bally Cor) about the medal prospects. He pointed to Mark and Charisma, saying: "There's the gold medal winner." I knew, after their Badminton performance, that Charisma and Mark had the ability to do very well, but I didn't really consider them as a gold medal prospect – gold medals were won by people from other countries, not by New Zealanders taking part in their first ever Olympic Games.

'I also had the good fortune of being part of the New Zealand team at Seoul, to witness a repeat performance of Los Angeles, except this time there was never any doubt who was favourite to win the gold medal. Mark and Charisma seemed to glide from start to finish, and there never appeared to be any doubt that they would do it. When I think of Charisma, I think of the partnership of Mark and the horse, because Charisma would not have won two gold medals without Mark as the jockey.'

called in to do our test, I put Podge into an extended trot down one side of the arena. He floated off in that amazing extended trot that he can do, and the whole grandstand erupted into applause. This startled him a bit, and he shot off, so I had to bring him back in hand and try to regain his concentration just before we entered the arena. I think without this disturbance he'd have done a better test, but he still did very well, and we ended up in fourth place.

I had already seen the cross-country course by then, and was a bit concerned by its size, though it wasn't as big as Badminton. It was a twisty course, and a lot of people thought that would be an advantage to me, because Podge is small and very nippy, but in fact he always seemed to go better on a big, open, galloping course. I wasn't too worried, though; he could handle corners very well, and it seemed that the most serious problem would be getting back within the time.

Los Angeles was an unusual event because it lasted for six days. After the dressage we had to box all the horses 120 miles to Del Mar, San Diego, for the cross-country. The horses were then given a rest day so that they could fully recover from yet another journey, and this provided the riders with a chance to study the cross-country in greater detail. It also gave us an excuse to have a bit of a party on the night we arrived in Del Mar because we didn't have to compete the next day.

The course had been built on a newly constructed golf course at Fairbanks Ranch, once the home of Douglas Fairbanks and Mary

Podge looking incredibly fit and healthy before an early morning canter at Santa Anita Racecourse. Without running-reins it was virtually impossible to hold him.

33

ABOVE: Podge in the dressage arena in Los Angeles. Though he lost his concentration moments before his test, he recovered well and finished in fourth place. RIGHT: Leaving the arena after his test, Podge relaxed and happy that it's all over.

Pickford. The developers at the site had brought in some 4 million cubic yards of earth and diverted the bed of the San Dieguito river – all for a golf course and country club! Although it made a nice setting for the cross-country, it can't have been easy to design a course on the site. There were only 140 acres to play with, and 20% of that was covered by lakes, so it wasn't surprising that the course was tight and twisty, and frequently doubled back on itself as it wound over and around the man-made hillocks of the golf course. The fences were beautifully constructed, and it seemed a pity that they all had to be broken down and removed straight after the event, but I suppose the golf club members wouldn't have taken too kindly to having these additional obstacles on their fairways.

On the day of the official briefing at Fairbanks, before the dressage had begun, the temperatures had been in the 90s, with not a breath of air, and most of the competitors were very worried about the conditions. The whole idea of holding the cross-country at Del Mar was that it was near the Pacific coast, where there was normally a good sea breeze to cool everyone down – but there wasn't much evidence of it on the day we first looked round the course. Much to everyone's relief, however, when the speed and endurance actually began at Del Mar the promised breeze had arisen, and it certainly improved things. As I was the last to go for the New Zealand team, Podge had to complete his speed and endurance in the hottest part of the day. It didn't seem to bother him, though: he was an absolute runaway on the steeplechase.

The going for the steeplechase phase was on hard, packed sand, which suited him perfectly. He wasn't an easy horse to hold at the best of times, and when he was really fit it was almost impossible. He was very fast and very strong, and four or five strides out from each fence he just took charge. In fact he stood back so far off some of the fences that a friend of mine, Pat Daley, who was watching, said afterwards: 'That horse shouldn't be eventing. He should be at Cheltenham.'

Podge finished the steeplechase at least 20 seconds under the time, with me swinging on him all the way to try and slow him down. It was good to know that he was fit and feeling so well, but I was a bit worried that he might have pulled all the strength and energy out of himself too soon. Halfway round the second phase of roads and tracks the competitors were allowed assistance to refresh the horses, and Podge had his mouth washed out and a bucket of water chucked over him. By the time we reached the ten-minute box at the start of the cross-country he was feeling bright and full of himself again.

When we set off on the cross-country I knew that if we were to be in the running we had to go clear within the time. The American rider Karen Stives, who had been two points ahead of us after the dressage, had already achieved a fast clear, putting her into the lead, and Ginny Leng had come home with only .4 of a time penalty. I expected both Lucinda Green and Bruce Davidson to get round within the time, which meant that I had to do the same.

Podge always set off on a cross-country course as if he meant business, and he would keep up a relentless gallop all the way. In Los Angeles the first few fences were straightforward and inviting, and he was going on strongly, so I had to just bring him under control for the fourth fence, the Mark of Zorro, so that we could get an accurate line for the corner. I took Fence 5, the Crescent Oxer, on the right hand side where the drop wasn't as big, and then we flew over the Open Water.

35

The Hayracks at Los Angeles were a very big fence. Podge is jumping them well but showing how he could sometimes twist his back end to clear a fence.

The seventh fence, the Bridge and Walkway, posed the first major problem. There was a slight downhill approach into the water, then there were two short strides to the jetty which you had to jump on to and then bounce out over some rails back into water. Because the strides to the jetty were so short, you had to come back almost to a trot as you approached the water. Quite a few horses had problems here – including Britain's 'Tiny' Clapham, who had a fall from Windjammer – and four other horses were retired at this fence. I brought Podge back to a slow canter, and he managed to fit in the two quick strides, jump on to the jetty and bounce out over the rail without any trouble.

The next three fences were fairly straightforward, though you were constantly riding up and down small hills, changing camber and often approaching fences at an awkward angle. I didn't get my line quite right through the Rattlesnake fence, and Podge was a bit far off the third element, but he got himself over it all right. Then came the Ghost Town,

which really did look like something out of an old Western movie, complete with its hotel, general store, livery and blacksmith. Most of us chose the direct route, jumping in through the picture window of the saloon bar, over a wide table in the middle, and then out over some rails. The striding was long, and you had to keep riding all the way to get through, but Charisma handled it well.

Watts Wall, an imposing upright, came next, followed by the Fairbanks. This fence had two main options, but very few people took the direct route. The New Zealand team had all decided that this route was very big and involved a lot of effort, so we came round to the left hand side of the fence and jumped across it, as did most others. The British team had posted one of their many supporters at this fence to time each horse. Those who went the direct route took about 12 seconds; the other route was taking around 24 seconds, depending on how neatly the horses negotiated it. Podge is so handy that he managed it in only 19 seconds: the fastest time of the day.

Two fences on from Fairbanks came The Waterfalls. Nobody really knew how this would ride, because we'd never before negotiated a fence with so much water, let alone jumped waterfalls! There were some fairly big rails into the water, which Podge jumped quite well, then a long stretch of water to the first waterfall. He popped up this without any trouble, then up another waterfall into the second pool where the water was really quite deep. You then had to turn left handed and jump out over a rail, but because of the deep water, most horses just sort of fell out. Charisma did much the same, but picked himself up and was off again, jumping well over the Hayracks and the Timber Wagon.

Then came the Ski Jump, where we had a bit of a narrow squeak. I had brought Podge back to a slow canter, and he popped happily off the edge of the drop, down a sharp hill with two strides to the second bank. But on his second stride, as he went to take off for the bank, he seemed to slip. His back feet went from under him and we skidded right into the base of the bank. Any less honest horse would have stopped, but somehow Podge managed to struggle up on to the bank and push himself off again.

We went on to the Osuna Brand, where Mary Hamilton and I were the only competitors to take the fast route. Even so, we had lost a bit of time in the middle section of the course and when I checked my watch at the three-quarter mark I realised we were slightly down on time. I gave Podge a kick, and after that he just flew home over the rest of the course, finishing way too fast. We were about half a minute under the optimum time – the fastest time of the day – and he still pulled up really well.

That was one of his great trade marks: he was always a remarkably sound horse and never came out stiff the day after the cross-country. I think it was because he had such good action that he never jarred himself. Whereas some horses seem to hammer into the ground at a gallop, Podge was really light and well-balanced, and moved beautifully. At all his three-day events we never had a moment's worry with

OPPOSITE: Podge gave this fence a good 'rub' and I'm looking down nervously to see that the rail is still in place. Los Angeles, 1984.

> ### Dr Bernd Springorum (FEI three-day event judge):
>
> 'I first met Charisma at the Los Angeles Olympics, where I was acting as coach for the German team. As usual, trainers and riders were sitting around the dressage arena, discussing judges' marks. We concentrated our different views on Oran, a marvellous Swiss horse with outstanding movement, but not always performing to the best of his ability. At this time I got my first impression of Charisma – a slightly limited mover (compared to a horse like Oran), but a horse that had been well educated in the principles of dressage, and who gave a solid, consistent performance. "Oran compared to Charisma" became an interesting headline for discussion on judges' courses.
>
> 'Instead of having a normal career, Charisma happened to meet a rider who obviously never asked more than his horse was ready to answer. The confidence of being able to answer every question, coupled with an active mind that doesn't try to escape from what is being asked, seem to me to be the basis of this horse's outstanding achievements. Horses like Charisma don't win just by clear rounds or good medium trots. They win because their fascinating personality stays untouched.'

him, and at Del Mar there was no question of his having problems at the inspection the day after the cross-country. Once that was over, the horses were boxed up again and driven back to Santa Anita Racecourse to await the final day's show jumping.

Podge's cross-country performance had left us in second place. The Swiss rider Hansueli Schmutz on Oran, who had been in the lead after the dressage, had had a fall on the cross-country; so, too, had the American Bruce Davidson, who had been lying second after the dressage, just ahead of Karen Stives. This meant that Karen, after her good cross-country round on Ben Arthur, was now in the lead, two points ahead of Podge and me.

The competitors show jumped in reverse order of merit, so I had a long wait before it was my turn. It was difficult to judge when would be the right time to bring Podge down from the stables, as the jumping was taking much longer than we'd anticipated. I was at the stadium watching the other horses and helping some of the other New Zealand riders, and twice I had to send someone back to the stables to tell Helen not to come down yet. Even when she did eventually arrive with Podge, she had to keep him waiting in the shade of the trees until it was time for me to start warming him up.

While I was in England I had been taking lessons in show jumping from Ted Edgar, and as he was out in Los Angeles with the British show jumping team he was able to give me some help when I was warming up. I was quite surprised when he started me off over a large oxer with a trot pole in front. He made me come round and trot into it. Podge

OPPOSITE: No mistakes this time as Podge picks up his feet. BELOW: The tension has gone and trainer Ted Edgar and I can discuss the merits of our show-jumping round.

knocked it down about four times, but I had such confidence in Ted that I assumed he knew what he was doing, and I didn't get too worried about it. Podge soon started jumping very well, so we moved through from the outside practice area into the main practice ring. I hopped off him for a few minutes, moved the saddle forward, got on again, and just gave him one pop over another fairly large oxer. He jumped it really well, so we just left it at that, and went into the ring.

The course was quite long, with well-spaced fences, and Ted had advised me to let him gallop on in between the jumps and just pick him up in front of each fence, rather than trying to keep him together the whole way round. That way it wouldn't tire him so much; it would keep the rhythm going and help get him round inside the time, which was quite tight. My biggest worry was the combination, the penultimate fence. As you approached it, it just looked like a mass of different coloured rails, and must have been very confusing for the horses.

Podge excelled himself. He jumped the course really well, and the only dodgy moment was when he rattled the first part of the combination. I was thrilled. He had gone into the Games as one of the dark horses of the field, and all I thought of when we'd finished our round was that we had won a silver medal, and that was tremendous.

Our clear round obviously put even more pressure on Karen Stives, who had the American team gold medal at stake as well as her individual medal. I didn't even watch most of her round because I'd already seen Ben Arthur warming up in the practice arena, and he was jumping like a stag. It seemed very unlikely that he would have a rail down.

There had been deadly silence in the arena while Karen was going round, and I decided to walk back along the alleyway to watch her over the last few fences. As I did – bump – down went the middle of the treble. I couldn't believe it.

I was immediately besieged by the press and then dragged off for television interviews and press conferences, which seemed to go on for ages. The nice thing about it was that everyone seemed really pleased that Podge had won – even the Americans. Questions came thick and fast, and I was in a bit of a daze, just hoping that my answers were making sense, and vaguely aware that I was missing a good party which was undoubtedly already in full swing back at the stables.

With the questions finally over, I thought I'd better telephone my parents. For some insane reason I assumed that they would not have

How the *New Zealand Times* recorded our first Olympic win.

Kiwi tears as 'I won for NZ'

BY ALEX VEYSEY

Mark Todd

BIG MARK drank champagne and little Charisma nuzzled tiredly away at oats,

Champagne and water flowed freely during a wild celebration after our success. Here Tiny Clapham receives a blast from Ginny Leng.

heard the news yet in New Zealand. But of course they had, and their telephone line was jammed with people ringing them up to congratulate them. It took me half an hour to get through, and when I did I couldn't get much sense out of them – they were all half drunk by then. Apparently the show jumping had been televised live, and friends, family and even a local television crew to film my parents' reactions, had gathered at home to watch the final show jumping.

That night we had a huge party in the stables. The New Zealand team, which had finished sixth, was, as usual, well prepared to celebrate whatever the result had been, and by the time I arrived the first case of Champagne had already disappeared. Soon everyone from every country had congregated there, and it was full steam ahead. There were water fights, races on golf carts, people having their clothes ripped off and being rolled in sand. It was all a delightful release of the tension that had built up in the weeks leading to the competition, and which was combined, for me, with the euphoria of winning an Olympic medal.

Podge was intrigued by the party, and spent most of the evening hanging over his stable door watching what was going on. The next day he was a bit tired and slept quite a lot, but it didn't take long for him to feel full of beans again, and Helen continued to ride him each day until it was time for him to come home.

I headed back to England before the end of the Games. I was all too conscious of Burghley looming up, and I felt that I had somewhat neglected the horse who I was due to ride there. With hindsight, it was stupid of me to go back before the end of the Games and to miss a once in a lifetime occasion. I should have stayed on to make the most of it and to take part in the closing ceremony. As it was, going back to England early didn't do me any good. Night Life fell on the cross-country course at Burghley, and I had to retire.

4 Troubled Times

Immediately after the Games, Podge's future came under threat. Fran Clark had decided to sell the horse, but she didn't seem at all inclined to negotiate a deal with my sponsors, Woolrest, so I was in serious danger of losing my ride on him. Mrs Clark claimed that she had had some fantastic offers for the horse, and that if we wanted him we would have to pay NZ$250,000. Bill Hall tried to come to an agreement with her, but got nowhere. Then Fran contacted event rider Lizzie Purbrick and offered the horse to her.

Lizzie Purbrick takes up the story:

'I had met Mrs Clark at Badminton in 1984. Reggie, my husband, had befriended her because she seemed a bit lost. She had come to Badminton to watch her horse compete, but didn't know anyone there, and Mark was too busy to look after her, so she got talking to Reggie and came back to the stables for a drink one evening. We didn't think any more about it until the following January when, completely out of the blue, we had a phone call from her offering to sell Charisma. She had managed to track us down at my brother-in-law's farm in New South Wales, where we were on holiday, to tell us that we were the only people she knew to whom she would like to sell the horse.

'At the time we were unaware of the publicity surrounding Charisma's future, but Reggie stalled for a while, saying that, yes, he'd love to buy the horse, and that it would make a wonderful birthday present for me! We than rang Mark in New Zealand to find out what on earth was going on. Mark was delighted that Fran had got in touch with us. She didn't know many people in the eventing world, and I think that's why she came to us. When we told Mark about her offer he was very keen to hatch a plot for us to buy Charisma and sell him straight on to Woolrest. We went along with the plan, because although I felt terribly embarrassed at having to deceive Fran about it all, it seemed to be the only way to ensure that Mark kept the ride on Charisma.

'When I arrived back in England after our holiday I arranged to meet Fran in London – at the Cavalry Club – to discuss terms and price. I remember the day vividly, because it was very cold and we had both had to struggle up the motorway in the snow. Fran may have smelt a rat; she was certainly very suspicious, and kept quizzing me about my intentions. I had to spin some story about getting a new sponsor who was willing to put up the money for me to buy Charisma, and to convince her that my interest was genuine. We agreed in principle that I would buy the horse for £50,000. (I had tried to negotiate a lower price for Woolrest, but when Fran began threatening to sell the horse to Japan, Bill Hall had told me just to settle the deal as quickly as possible!)

'Fran insisted that I try the horse before finalising things, so I had to arrange to meet her the following day at Melanie Duff's yard, where Charisma was spending the winter. Melanie knew exactly what was going on – but even so the last thing I wanted to do was drive through the snow to Swindon to ride the horse, especially as I was three months pregnant at the time. (I certainly hadn't told Fran that.) Luckily, that night there was a really heavy snowstorm, and the next day the M4 Motorway in Wiltshire was completely blocked, which made it impossible for me to get there. Fran was already booked on a flight back to New Zealand that evening, and fortunately she just signed the contract and left. It was a great relief.

'Woolrest then paid the £50,000 into my account at Hungerford (which caused a good deal of excitement for my bank manager), and two days later I wired the money to New Zealand. I'm now very proud to think that I actually owned Charisma for about three days, but the saddest thing is that I never had a real ride on him. Mark very kindly offered to let me try him out, but it was one of those things that I never got round to doing. Still, I was delighted to have helped keep Mark and Charisma together. It would have been tragic if their partnership had come to an end so soon.'

Lizzie's deal with Fran was the best thing that could have happened to me. I had been in New Zealand while the wrangling over Podge's future was at its height, and had decided that, if I couldn't keep him, there wouldn't be much point in returning to England. I would sell Night Life and stay at home. But after the complicated negotiations between Fran, Lizzie and Woolrest, Bill Hall said that Podge was now mine, and that I could keep him as long as I wanted. He also extended Woolrest's sponsorship for another year. He was a tremendous man, and so generous; I was incredibly lucky to have him backing me at that time.

Lizzie Purbrick with her son Arthur. Lizzie's skilful negotiations enabled Podge and me to stay together when his owner decided to sell up.

5 Moving Forward Again

I returned to England at the beginning of 1985 to find Podge in great form. Helen had already begun walking exercise to get him fit, and by the start of the spring season he was going really well. He won all his one-day events before Badminton – Crookham, Aldon and Brigstock.

Although we went to Badminton as Olympic Champions, I wasn't at all affected by other people's expectations of us. I do sometimes put pressure on myself, but external pressures have never really bothered me. I wanted Podge to win, and I felt reasonably confident that he could, even though this was the biggest track he'd ever done. It was certainly more difficult than the Los Angeles and 1984 Badminton courses, and, added to that, there was a very strong field of competitors. A lot of the Olympic riders had brought their horses over to England to compete.

Three of the American team who had won the gold medal in LA were there (Karen Stives with Ben Arthur, Torrance Fleischmann with Finvarra, Bruce Davidson with JJ Babu), and so were all the British Olympic team members, with the exception of Lucinda Green and Regal Realm. Altogether there were fourteen riders at Badminton who had competed in Los Angeles the previous summer, so it was a bit like an Olympic replay.

Podge did a good dressage test, and finished second to Torrance Fleischmann. I knew she would be difficult to beat, and the next day she and Finvarra had a great cross-country round, finishing inside the time, despite having to tackle the course in a snowstorm. For some reason, though, Torrance had misjudged her timing on the steeplechase, and had incurred 2.4 penalties, which was enough to allow me and Podge to slip ahead.

The weather was appalling that day. Podge and I had been on Phase C (roads and tracks) during the worst of the snowstorm, but fortunately it had stopped by the time we set out on the cross-country. Although the ground was a bit soft – not Podge's favourite going – he jumped really well. In fact, he pulled so hard round the first part of the course I vowed that from then on I would use a metal snaffle when I rode him cross-country, rather than the rubber bit that I'd always had him in before.

We finished the course clear within the time, putting us into the lead, but the scores were very close: there were only four points separating me, Torrance and Ginny Leng, who was in third place with Night Cap. Torrance nearly fell at the first part of the treble when Finvarra misjudged his stride, and they had two rails down. Podge then jumped one of his best show jumping rounds ever; he hardly touched a thing until he came to the final treble. There was an oxer in, one stride to an

ABOVE: Podge bows to the judges in a near-perfect halt at Badminton, 1985.

RIGHT: Badminton, 1985. Podge at full steam in the cross-country, and me with the proverbial double handful. Here, he is wearing a rubber snaffle, but some time later I changed to a thin metal one to help exert some control.

Podge jumping brilliantly in and out of the water complex at Badminton, 1985. I think this is one of the most difficult fences ever built at the lake.

ABOVE LEFT: A wonderful expression on Podge's face as he clears one of the earlier obstacles in the show jumping at Badminton. Knocking the very last fence down, in what was otherwise one of his best show-jumping rounds, relegated us to second place. ABOVE RIGHT: Posing for Kit Houghton.

upright, and then two very short strides to another oxer, which is just the sort of fence he finds really difficult when he has to shorten in the middle of a combination. He flicked the front pole off the final element on his way up, and that was it. Ginny had gone clear, and she won it. Once again, Podge had finished in second place.

He then had a short break until the summer. I decided not to compete in a three-day event with him in the autumn because the 1986 World Championships were quite early on in the following season, and I thought it would be best to keep him fresh. We entered five one-day events before the end of that year and, with the exception of Dauntsey, where he had a fall at the last fence on the cross-country, won them all.

A week after Dauntsey we went to Gatcombe, where the conditions were so bad that I nearly withdrew him. Heavy rain had been falling since the early morning on cross-country day, and it wasn't long before the whole place was inches deep in liquid mud. A lot of people decided not to run their horses, but I had a ride in the first section on Michaelmas Day, who handled the course really well, and I realised that although the ground was wet it wasn't heavy. We were going through the slop on top, and getting quite a good footing underneath, so I thought Podge would probably be all right. He obviously thought so, too, and scorched round the course with no trouble. We'd had a fence down in the show jumping, and so lost the advantage of a good dressage test, and when we set out on the cross-country we were on an equal score with Jonquil Sainsbury and Hassan. Jonquil, who went ahead of us, certainly didn't hang around – but, luckily, Podge finished the course just one second faster, and we won by a whisker.

Gatcombe was followed by another win at Bourton before the last event of the season, Castle Ashby. Podge was really full of himself there, and riding him in for the dressage was a nightmare. The start of the cross-country wasn't far away from the dressage area, and Podge, well aware of what was going on, flatly refused to settle down. I rode him in for about three-quarters of an hour, but he was still careering around the place, and in the end I'd virtually given up any hope of doing a decent test and thought we'd just have to go in and muddle our way through. But as soon as he entered the arena he completely changed, as if to say: 'Right, here I am, I'll behave now.' He produced a really outstanding test, and landed up with a score of 15, the lowest mark ever given for an Advanced one-day test.

After that it was easy. Despite having a rail down in the show jumping and 7 time faults on the cross-country, we were so far ahead of anyone else that we still won the competition with 15 points to spare.

Podge at full stretch putting in a very fast round in wet conditions to win his first British Open title at Gatcombe, 1985.

Our final score was 27, and second to us was Mike Tucker's General Bugle with 42.

Castle Ashby was the end of a remarkable season for Podge. Apart from the mistake at Dauntsey, he had won every one-day event he ran in that year (i.e. seven wins in all), and he had finished second at Badminton – an exceptional record by any standards.

1986 began in the same vein, with a win at Aldon, the only one-day event we could compete in before the horses had to go into quarantine for the World Championships at Gawler, Australia. Podge went to Wylye with the British horses, which was very handy as it was just down the road from me. By then I had my horses stabled at Cholderton, near Salisbury, so I could drive over to Wylye every day to exercise Podge.

The horses were in quarantine for a month, but fortunately the facilities at Wylye were so good that Podge didn't get bored. We had a practice event about a week before the horses were due to leave for Australia, just dressage and cross-country,.and Podge went like a lunatic again. He always pulled much more at home than he did in competition, and after working for a few weeks around the grounds at Wylye he'd got to know the place really well and obviously felt completely at home. So he tore round the cross-country course there, going much too fast, and hit one of the fences really hard. His stifle swelled up quite badly, but luckily it didn't develop into anything more serious and it settled down again soon after he arrived in Australia.

Podge and the other horses left England on the last day of Badminton, where I was riding a horse called Any Chance. I finished fifth on him, and later that week flew out to Australia to join Podge. Everyone had been really worried about the journey for the horses because it was so far, but I wasn't too concerned. Podge had handled the flight from New Zealand to England so well that I didn't think he'd have any problems with this one, and, besides, although the total flying time was 36 hours, it can sometimes take at least that long to get to a European event in a horse box.

The next ten days were spent in quarantine at Torrens Island, which was rather tedious, because there really wasn't much space in which to exercise the horses, and we were glad to move out of there to the main base at Roseworthy Agricultural College. We then had the option of competing in a one-day event at Reynella, and as Podge hadn't had a proper outing since Aldon nearly eight weeks earlier, I thought it would

Ian Stark (Olympic silver medallist, Seoul):

'Charisma is undoubtedly one of the most amazing little horses we will ever see in our lifetime. You don't think of Toddy without the name Charisma springing to mind.

'Like many people, I wasn't over-impressed when I first saw Charisma during the build-up to Badminton in 1984. But of course we were all proved wrong. I remember when we were in quarantine at Wylye before the World Championships in 1986. Charisma showed that he was second to none for sheer toughness and stamina. On practice gallops he just kept going and going . . .

'It was almost as if Charisma decided which events were worth winning, and which were not. He always seemed to rise to the occasion at the really important ones.'

be a good idea to run him.

It was a bit of a risk doing an event so close to the World Championships, and a lot of the riders decided not to run their horses on the cross-country, but Podge always went better in a big event if he'd had a competition beforehand to take the edge off him. The chances of him damaging himself were quite slim because he was basically such a sound horse, and although he tended to bolt round the smaller courses he looked after himself. If he did make a mistake it was usually because I had tried to interfere. The Reynella course wasn't particularly testing, and Podge won the competition. We then had a few more days to prepare for the championships.

The atmosphere in the dressage arena at Gawler didn't really suit Podge. There were big stands all around the arena, with nobody in them, and there were masses of flags about the place, flapping in the wind. As soon as we came in to do our test there was a constant whir of cameras – I suppose because we were the Olympic champions – and the whole thing unsettled Podge. He was just a bit on edge all the way through his test, and I couldn't really ride him the way I like to in a dressage test. We ended up second to Torrance Fleischmann and Finvarra, and it was the last time that Podge was ever beaten in a dressage test in a three-day event.

The cross-country course was a strange mixture of very big fences and some much smaller ones, with a huge hill in the middle. The terrain was quite tough, and a lot of horses didn't really seem fit enough to tackle it, but I knew Podge would be all right. He'd settled in well in his temporary home and had soon come back to peak fitness after the journey.

As there weren't too many competitors at Gawler, I saw only three horses on the closed circuit TV before I set out on the speed and endurance. Not one of them went clear through the water, so it didn't do much to help me confirm which was the best route to take. I had decided to go to the left of the shorter option: which proved to be a mistake.

Winning at Reynella, just days away from the World Championships at Gawler. Podge used to need a few runs before a three-day event to burn off some of his exuberance. He would often take charge in front of a fence and stand off from wherever he liked.

Annoyed by his fall at the water
(see overleaf), Podge attacks this big
parallel, the last element of the
State Banks, at Gawler, 1986. Look
where his knees are!

The point of no return – Gawler, 1986. For a split second I thought he would keep his feet, but a ducking was inevitable. I felt that I had let him down and robbed him of the chance to become Olympic and World Champion.

The start of the course was a bit dodgy because it was downhill on slippery ground, and with Podge raring to go – as he always was when we set out on the cross-country – I had to try and steady him back as much as possible. I was particularly concerned about the second fence, a very upright logpile, which had caused one or two horses to tip up, but Podge jumped it well. At the Jubilee J's, where Ian Stark had had his slip-up, I had opted for a different route, going from left to right, so that I didn't have to do a sharp turn in between the two rails, and Podge didn't have any problems there.

The water complex, Dead Man's Pass, was at Fence 9. Before I'd set off on the cross-country I knew that Tinks Pottinger, for our New Zealand team, had jumped the right hand route in the water successfully, so I

ABOVE LEFT: Podge showing his objection to being photographed when having a bath. ABOVE RIGHT: Schooling on a hot day. LEFT: Podge looking decidedly pleased with his performance after the dressage test at Gawler. I was decidedly peeved. BELOW: After the long climb up the Gawler hill, Podge was still galloping and jumping effortlessly.

RIGHT: A relaxed moment for both of us at Luhmühlen, 1986. This was so typical of him. Although completely at ease he was still totally alert to his surroundings. BELOW: Luhmühlen, 1986. Worried about what happened in the water at Gawler, I over-rode him on to this bank and nearly paid the penalty. He powered over the rail off the bank, firing me up his neck.

assumed that Podge could also do the same. The first part of the fence was a rail followed by one long stride to a log with a drop into water, then a bounce to another rail. Most of the other riders had gone for the same option, but had jumped it further to the right, where the gap between the log and the rail in the water was wider, so that they just had room to shuffle in a short stride between the two fences. I think if I'd done that I'd have probably got away with it, but instead I went to the left and Podge just wasn't big enough to manage the stretch for the bounce. He bellied the rail coming out, and we were both submerged in the water. If Tinks hadn't jumped to the far left so well on the big-striding Volunteer, and if I'd been better informed, I would probably have taken the fence on the right hand side, and it might have been a very different story. But I didn't, and that was that.

Once you've had a fall – particularly when you've been in with a good chance – it's very difficult to pick yourself up and find the motivation to complete the rest of the course, and this was only Fence 9. We'd both been completely immersed; everything was wet and slippery; and Podge had water down his ears, which annoyed him. But I knew we had to get going again quickly; it was still important for the team that we should go clear over the rest of the course, as one of our members, Merran Hain, had had two falls. So I gave Podge a couple of cracks with the stick, just to get his mind on the job and say: 'Come on. We've got to carry on.' The next fence, the double brush oxer, was big and imposing, and it needed attacking. Fortunately, Podge just got on with the job and jumped it well.

We went round the remainder of the course without incident – one minute jumping big, testing fences, the next skipping over some ineffectual, nondescript types of jump. After Fence 13 came the long climb up a steep hill which went on for about a mile. This was the part of the course that really cooked some of the horses, and one or two stopped at the relatively straightforward Brewery Drays near the top of the hill just because they were out of puff. Podge finished the course well, though I hadn't been particularly anxious to go fast. Once we'd had the fall, the main thing was to get back safely, and at least we'd achieved that. We had time-faults anyway, because of the fall.

Nevertheless there had been so much carnage on the cross-country course that despite the addition of my 82 penalty points the New Zealand team went into the lead. Tinks Pottinger and Trudy Boyce both had terrific rounds and went into first and third places respectively, so we looked set to win two individual medals as well as the team gold. But all our hopes fell apart the next day when Tinks' horse failed the final vet inspection and had to be withdrawn from the competition. Our team placing dropped to fourth, and after that I have to admit that I slightly lost interest in the competition, though it was great to see Trudy win the individual silver medal.

Podge had a couple of fences down in the show jumping, and we finished in tenth place – not bad for a World Championship, but we should have done better. Nobody has ever won the Olympics and the World Championships, and we had been so near and yet so far. I was really disappointed, as I thought Gawler would probably be Podge's last international championship. There had even been talk of sending him straight home to New Zealand. If he'd won, I might well have done that, but I didn't want him to go out on that sort of note, and more than anything else I wanted to have another crack at Badminton with him.

When we arrived back from Gawler, Podge was on such good form that I decided to take him to Luhmühlen in West Germany. The event was at the beginning of August, only two months after our return to England, so Podge was the first of the championship horses to run in another three-day event, but he was so well that there didn't seem any point in turning him out for a rest.

He performed one of the best dressage tests that he'd ever achieved at a three-day event, and we were given three 10s in the marks, finishing with a score of 29.2. It's quite exceptional for a horse to score fewer than 30 points in an international three-day event, and Podge must be one of the few who has ever achieved it.

The cross-country course was big, but reasonably straightforward,

and we just had one dicey moment at the water. I think it was mainly because I was panicking about having had a fall in Gawler, and I over-rode it. We had to jump into the water over a big log, run through the water and up on to a bank, bounce over a rail into water again, and then after a few strides jump up on to another bank, one stride and over a rail. I rode him too strongly at the bank in the middle, and he bounded up on to it, flew off over the rail and sort of screwed in mid-air as he was coming down to land. I ended up hanging off the side of him, but somehow managed to stay put and he just kept going. Apart from that, he gave me a really good ride.

We had a rail down in the show jumping, but so did the two riders behind me, Betty Overesch, from Germany, and Lucinda Green, and

Despite his previous ducking at Gawler, Charisma shows his courage by confidently jumping into the water at Luhmühlen. I wasn't feeling so sure! (See also page 58.)

anyway we had a big enough lead over them that we could have afforded another fence down and still won. For the first time in my life I was also in a winning team. The FEI had given us permission to enter a Commonwealth team, and Lucinda Green, Ian Stark and I swept the board, finishing nearly 100 points ahead of Italy, with Germany in third. Not surprisingly, the FEI didn't allow us to form a team like that again.

It had been a really good event and Podge had gone brilliantly, but the best thing about it was that Carolyn and I became engaged.

After the World Championships in Gawler, Woolrest had terminated their sponsorship with me. I had known that this would be happening – Bill Hall had already supported me for a year longer than he'd originally planned – and at the Olympia Horse Show the previous December I had mentioned the matter to Linda Warren, who was then working for British Equestrian Promotions. Although I didn't know it at the time, Merrill Lynch had already been having discussions with BEP about sponsorship, but hadn't found anything suitable. When Linda suggested that they might sponsor me, they thought that was an excellent

Tinks Pottinger (member of New Zealand's Olympic team):

'I first competed with Mark and Charisma in the team for the World Championships in Gawler in 1986. Although not that successful in Australia, Mark and Charisma still put up an unforgettable performance. After falling at the water, Mark wasted no time in remounting, to finish with one of the fastest times and helping to keep the New Zealand team in the lead – albeit temporarily.

'It was in Australia that Mark suggested I take my two advanced horses to the UK. With the help of sponsors I was able to spend the best part of two years at Cholderton with Mark and Carolyn, and it was here that I really appreciated what a special, if somewhat frustrating, little horse Charisma was. At times I could have sworn he understood every bit of what was said to him, and on many occasions his thought processes were so obvious that it was easy to imagine what he was saying in return.

'I still smile when I remember the times when Mark used to "loose-school" Podge over show jumps in the indoor school. I was never sure who was giving whom the lesson: regardless of how well he jumped, Podge would always stop by the exit, turn and look at Mark, half quizzically, half defiantly, as if to say: "I thought that was pretty good, Dad. Didn't you?"

'Gallop days were another source of entertainment if you went with Mark and Podge. My horse Graphic, an ex-racehorse, was by no means slow, but Podge invariably left a clean pair of heels. And if you think you have been on a "puller", try Podge. You wouldn't find weight training necessary after some fast canter work with him.

'I feel privileged to have known so personally not only Charisma, but also his equally famous jockey: to have seen their highs and lows, all taken with graciousness and modesty. Although a Kiwi myself and probably biased, I feel that they are the greatest combination the eventing world has ever seen, and we Kiwis are certainly grateful to them for putting New Zealand eventing where it is today.'

idea – much to my surprise and relief. They agreed to pay the expenses of six horses, two of them Advanced, so by the time we went to Luhmühlen in August I was riding under their banner.

Podge competed in one more one-day event that year, at Thirlestane Castle, where he came second, and was then turned out for his winter rest. My plan was to bring him up in the spring for our third attempt at Badminton. I was convinced that it would be third time lucky, and that in 1987 it would be Podge's turn to win, instead of coming second again.

The preparations had gone well, and by April Podge was as fit and well as he had ever been. Tinks Pottinger and Trudy Boyce had come over from New Zealand, and were staying with us at Cholderton. We were on the verge of loading the horses into the box to set off for Badminton when we had a phone call to say it had been cancelled because the ground was too wet. We were devastated. Tinks and Trudy had come over specially to compete, and I had pinned my hopes on Podge winning at last.

Podge never did get his third chance to run there. If he had, perhaps he would have succeeded, but it seemed that he was destined never to win the Whitbread Trophy.

Badminton's cancellation meant that we had to hurriedly rethink our programme. I took Podge off to France to the three-day event in Saumur, which, as in Luhmühlen, he led from start to finish, and even jumped a clear round in the show jumping.

Knifing over the big hedge at Saumur in 1987, where Podge led from start to finish.

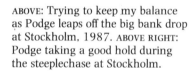

ABOVE: Trying to keep my balance as Podge leaps off the big bank drop at Stockholm, 1987. ABOVE RIGHT: Podge taking a good hold during the steeplechase at Stockholm.

In June we went to Stockholm, and again, he went into the lead after the dressage. The steeplechase course was on heavy sand, which was the sort of ground Podge hates. Only one or two horses managed to finish within the time, and Podge was a couple of seconds over, which was unusual for him. Stockholm was the only event where he ever had time faults on the 'chase. He went fast and clear cross-country, to keep us in the lead, but then the show jumping was on the same sort of ground as the steeplechase. Podge's show jumping has never been that reliable, but at least on hard ground he was usually reasonably good. If it was slightly muddy or deep he was hopeless, and the sand at Stockholm was probably the worst possible going for him. He had four fences down, and we dropped from first to sixth.

I took him to Burghley in the autumn of 1987. He'd had a good run at Rotherfield Park one-day event, which he'd won, and at Burghley he once more went into the lead after the dressage. I'd been a bit worried about him before Burghley because he had developed a habit of flicking his head about when I was schooling him. He'd never done it before, and I wondered if his sinuses were giving him more trouble than we realised – or perhaps it was just the flies bothering him. Fortunately, when he came to do his dressage at Burghley he didn't shake his head at all, and performed quite a good test. Nevertheless, I'd decided that after the event I would get his sinuses checked again.

He felt tremendous on the cross-country, and I had one of the best

Lucinda Green (past World and European Champion):

'With the breadth of forehead and the bright brown eyes, this little horse obviously has a huge brain and personality. His way of going is characterised by the lightness of his step. The agility with which he moves must be his greatest asset, for it maintained his soundness through a long career of very fast cross-country rounds.

'One of my most lasting memories of Charisma and possibly the most encouraging one for others, is that his style of jumping is not classical, and he gives the appearance over show jumps of not being over-scopey or over-cautious.'

Best foot forward. Burghley, 1987.

rides on him that I have ever had. All the way round he felt really comfortable and jumped the fences easily. Sometimes when horses get older (Podge was fifteen by then) they start to struggle a bit over the fences and don't really gallop on and do the job, but Podge just felt like he had always felt. It was a big course that year as well, and only six horses got round clear within the time – four of them were ridden by New Zealanders!

I had a second ride on a horse called Wilton Fair who I'd taken over as an Intermediate at the beginning of the year. He'd had a consistent season and had qualified very quickly, so although I thought he would be all right at Burghley it was a big test for him. However, he handled the cross-country really well, and at the end of the day he and Podge occupied the first two places.

LEFT: We went a bit deep to this fence and Podge had to climb out of trouble. Burghley, 1987. ABOVE: 1987 Burghley winner, Wilton Fair, and Charisma, runner-up, matching strides during their lap of honour.

Podge had a fence in hand over Wilton Fair, so I thought that, finally, he was going to win a major three-day event in England. But it was not to be. Wilton Fair jumped a clear in the show jumping, and Podge had two rails down. The first mistake was probably my fault. I was being over-cautious, and I checked a bit too much going into two related fences. The second of these was a wall which he wouldn't normally hit, but he had this one down. Then the next rail that we had down was his fault. It was a combination, which he never likes, and he was just careless.

It was nice to have won Burghley, but I still felt that it should have been the other way round, with Podge in first place and Wilton Fair second. Podge deserved to have one victory at a three-day event in England, instead of always finishing second.

6 Double Gold

After Burghley a lot of people thought that I would retire Charisma. He was fifteen, already quite old for a three-day event horse, and it would have been a fairly good note to end on. But it was exactly at that stage that I began to think seriously of taking him to Seoul. He had felt so good on the cross-country at Burghley – just as strong and fit and agile as ever – and I made up my mind that if he came back all right the following year we'd aim him at the Olympics.

So in 1988 we brought him back up into work on the basis that he would be going to Seoul. There was quite a bit of pressure on me at the time for wanting to take an 'old' horse to the Olympics. It wasn't helped by one or two recent instances of older horses dropping dead in competition; earlier in the year John Whitaker's nineteen-year-old Ryan's Son had collapsed in the ring at Hickstead and had died soon afterwards. People were very conscious that it was asking a lot of a sixteen-year-old to travel to Seoul for the Olympics, especially when he would be ridden in the three-day event – the toughest of the equestrian competitions.

I kept an open mind on it all. As I had a reserve horse, Bahlua, I didn't have to rely on Podge. The decision was always going to be that I would run him only if he was 100% fit and well and if I felt that he could do himself justice at the Games. If there was any doubt, I wouldn't start him, and he would be retired straight away. Whatever happened, Seoul was going to be his last competition. By then he would be half way home, and could just carry on back to New Zealand.

I decided not to enter him for Badminton in 1988 because I thought that at his age two big championships in a year might be asking a bit much. I very nearly changed my mind, though. We had already got him three-day event fit in the spring, because with old horses I think you have to keep them up to the mark. Podge was feeling exceptionally well, anyway, and at Brockenhurst – his second one-day event of the season – he gave me a terrible time. He was fine in the dressage, and we went into the lead, but he was like a lunatic in the show jumping, running all over the place, and had two fences down. I then had one of the most hairy cross-country rides I have ever known, because he bolted the whole way round: he was just so fit and well. When I arrived home I nearly rang up the Badminton office to see if I could get a late entry, but in the end decided to stick to my original plan. The only thing to do with him at that stage was to let him down again before he blew a gasket – he was much too fit for one-day events.

When he came up at the end of the summer he was still feeling exceptionally well. In fact, he was on tremendous form all through

Splashing through the water at Belton Park Horse Trials, 1988.

Happy and confident in the cross-country at Holker Hall in 1988.

1988. At the beginning of August I took him to Holker Hall, where the riders shortlisted for the British team were having their final selection trial. Podge hadn't run in a competition since Brockenhurst, four months earlier, and, again, he was just like a thing possessed. He blew up in the dressage: the only time he had really done this with me. He skittled four show jumps, and then went reasonably well across country. After that performance I think most people thought he was past it. My other horse, Bahlua, had finished second to Ginny Leng's Murphy Himself in the other Advanced section, so people assumed that I would ride him rather than Charisma in the Olympics. But I knew Charisma well enough to realise that the main reason for his appalling performance was simply that he was too fresh.

None of the British team members ran their horses on the cross-country at Gatcombe the following week because they were worried that they might injure themselves. But Charisma desperately needed another run. It was going to be about five weeks before we tackled the cross-country at Seoul, and although it was taking a slight risk, I wanted him to have this extra outing. I had given him a lot of work the week after Holker Hall, and by the time we arrived at Gatcombe he was a different horse, though still a little bit over the top. I think the

Lorna Clarke (international event rider):

'Throughout the years of this partnership I was always telling Mark that he should have given Charisma to me, as he was much too small for him, but he wouldn't have it and went ahead and won two gold medals on him. I think he very much proved a point that I have always believed in – that you don't need a big horse to do the "eventing" job. The smaller ones are quick-thinking, quick-acting, have plenty of scope and speed, and less to go wrong with them, as Charisma has proved over and over again.

'He is the sort of little horse we need in the sport. Not only is he brilliant but he has "charisma", character and a personality that appeals to the crowds without whom we wouldn't have our sport at all. He is the "Stroller" of the eventing world.

'I remember, when in training at Wylye for the World Championships in Australia, we would be schooling on the flat in the indoor school and Mark would come in and start doing flying changes every second and make the rest of us sick. I commended Mark on his riding, and he never actually admitted that the horse had reached Medium level dressage before he started riding him!

'I think one of the nicest things about Mark and Charisma is that they are both such personalities in their own right. Everyone was always behind them and enjoyed watching their partnership, as they always seemed to be "as one". There can't have been a single person in Korea who didn't want them to win on the show jumping day. Together they sum up all that is best in our sport: talent, courage, ability, combined with understanding and generosity. The little horse gives all that he has got (except, of course, when he is taking the "mick" out of Mark, as at Holker Hall in 1988), and Mark is a true friend to his horse.

'Mark's partnership with Charisma is something the rest of us would love to emulate, but are very unlikely to do so. Charisma will have to go down in history as the "greatest little horse eventing has ever known", and probably ever will know.'

atmosphere there helped to get him in the right frame of mind. Because he enjoyed performing in front of big crowds, he obviously thought it was worth making an effort. We led in the dressage, went clear show jumping, and then had one of the fastest cross-country rounds.

Our win at Gatcombe, by ten points from Robert Lemieux and The Poser, confirmed that Charisma was on form, and when I was asked by a reporter if I would be taking Charisma to Seoul, I replied: 'Yes, and he'll be even better there.' I felt confident that he would be, because I knew that I hadn't given him enough work. Most of my time had been spent preparing Bago, the horse that I was to ride in the Olympic show jumping competition, and I knew that once Podge arrived in Seoul and I had done more work with him, he would be even better.

I was so pleased that Podge had won Gatcombe. It was his last event in England, so he was leaving on a good note, and it was as if to say: 'I'm not finished yet.'

Podge proved he wasn't a spent force by winning the British Open Championships at Gatcombe, 1988, his last event in Britain.

He travelled out to Seoul quite happily. That was always one of the great things about him: you could take him anywhere, do anything with him, and he never fretted or worried. As long as he had something to eat, he would settle down straight away. The flight was only fourteen hours, six fewer than the normal travelling time, because the planes carrying the Olympic horses had been given permission to fly over Moscow. They went on a newly-built plane that was better equipped than the DC8s which had taken them to Los Angeles, so there were no problems over temperature control, and loading was easy.

When it had first been announced that the 1988 Games were to be in Korea, I think that most people in the equestrian world had serious misgivings about shipping horses to a country that has a history of political unrest and no real background in equestrian sports or horsemanship. Added to that, no one seemed to know what diseases there were out there, what quarantine would be necessary for the horses and, indeed, whether the horses would be allowed to return from Seoul when it was all over.

Carolyn and I were lucky enough to be able to visit Korea on our way back from New Zealand to England in February '88, to assess the facilities. We were amazed by what we found. The Koreans are great copiers, and they had done their homework by travelling the world collecting ideas from all the leading establishments, and had then moulded the best of them into one fantastic unit at the Kwa'Chon Equestrian Park. This was all very reassuring, and once the FEI had sorted out the quarantine regulations we felt much happier about going out there.

There were seven horses going to Seoul from our yard at Cholderton – Podge, Bahlua, and my show jumper Bago; Tinks' two horses, Volunteer and Graphic; and two others belonging to the Spanish rider Santé de la Roche, who was based with us. We were given permission to use the bottom yard at Cholderton as quarantine stables, which was very convenient, and the horses spent three weeks there before their flight. Once in Seoul they had only another 36 hours in quarantine before moving into their permanent stables at Kwa'Chon, which was about half an hour's drive from the centre of the city of Seoul.

It's always exciting to go to a country that is completely different from your own, and Korea was no exception. The first thing that hit you, almost literally, was the erratic driving of the locals. Everyone had stories of narrow escapes at the hands of our drivers. You soon learned not to sit near the front of the shuttle buses, as that proved to be too terrifying; at the back you couldn't see what was going on. Most of the time, the buses had a motorbike police escort and we seemed to have the right to shoot red lights, at will, turn where and when we liked, and go as fast as we wanted. On one occasion, as we approached a busy four-way intersection, our intrepid motorcycle police escort, undaunted by the red light facing us, switched on his siren, took both hands off his handlebars and held them up in the air, and, without a moment's hesitation, barrelled on through. Traffic all around screeched to a halt as we sailed majestically on.

Shopping in the markets was a fascinating experience. Everything was so incredibly cheap that you ended up buying things that you didn't really need, simply because they *were* so cheap. Here, the Koreans' great ability to copy was to the fore again – Roebuck shoes, Gucci bags, Rolex watches, Cartier briefcases, Pierre Cardin fashion garments – you name it, they could make it. There was no shortage of nightlife, either. One evening spent drinking the local rice wine was nearly enough to put me off alcohol for the rest of my life. One of the French team who was with us that night didn't turn up until 2 o'clock the next afternoon and couldn't remember anything from the previous evening – or at least he wasn't letting on.

All the teams – from athletes to yachtsmen – were housed in new apartment blocks in the city centre, so we in the New Zealand contingent had a block to ourselves. The management had learnt from our behaviour in Los Angeles that it would be best to put the equestrian team on their own floor, so that they wouldn't disturb the 'serious' athletes. Some of them couldn't believe that we could smoke and have parties and still compete successfully. But they were all great. The medical team used to provide us with ice for our drinks and we even devised a new cocktail out there called 'Sustagin'. One night we ran out of tonic for the gin, and were in dire straits. We had been given a lime-flavoured electrolyte replacer, Sustalyte, to help prevent dehydration in the heat, so came up with the idea of gin, Sustalyte and water – a great hit. The Irish, never slow to sniff out a watering hole, soon found a little bar just outside the village compound, and a few late nights were spent there.

A lot of people complained about the food, but it really wasn't too bad. You had to avoid the local dishes like the plague, but catering for so many people is no mean feat, and most of the food had to be imported. We usually had a reasonable choice, and, anyway, I was watching my weight, so I had to be quite careful what I ate. In fact the weight came off really easily, and I got down to about 11st 3lb, so that I had to use my saddle to weigh-in after the cross-country, as I had done in Los Angeles.

What struck me most about the competition in Seoul was that there were so many similarities to Los Angeles. The show jumping and dressage were held on a racecourse surrounded by flags and stands, with a backdrop of mountains reminiscent of Santa Anita. The cross-country was at a separate site, so that, as at San Diego, the horses had to travel there from their main base; the course was built on undulating ground, not a golf course this time, but you still found yourself constantly going up or down a slight rise, or round the side of a hill. And it was hot – hotter than expected for September.

Claus Erhorn (*Olympic three-day event rider, West Germany*):

'I have been on many trips with "Podge", including Los Angeles, Gawler and Seoul. He never seemed to show any signs of getting older, and at every event he looked as if he'd just popped out of a Christmas cracker. At the same time he knew his job inside out; he knew when to show the elegance of a gentleman in the dressage arena, and the strength of a fighter on the cross-country. There was never any doubt that he would complete an event, but with a less skilled rider on board I'm sure he wouldn't have collected so many medals.

'At the World Championships in Gawler I remember how my mare, Fair Lady, and Podge were desperately in love. Sami, my groom, and Helen always had to arrange for both horses to be turned out in separate paddocks at the same time, otherwise there were tears!'

Podge also seemed to sense the familiarity of the setting and atmosphere. When he got there you could almost feel him looking around the place and saying to himself: 'Okay, here we are again. I know what this is all about.'

Right from the word go he just settled down and got on with his work. He was going as well, if not better, than ever. When we were doing canter work around the track I was flat out just to hold him. People watching were amazed; they just couldn't believe it when they saw this little horse screeching along with me virtually out of control. Everyone commented on how well he looked, and that he didn't look like an old horse. He certainly never *felt* like an old horse.

Sometimes you just have a feeling about a competition, and although I was nervous in Seoul, I had a certain sense that this was the right time – everything about it was right. The horse felt great, he seemed really

---

Wally Niederer (vet to the New Zealand team):

'He was very well named – Charisma he certainly has. One of the most startling things about him even today is that he is as sound as a bell. I believe this is totally due to his very good conformation and his compact 15.3 size – and of course his athletic ability. From a veterinary point of view, Charisma is a dream to work with. Firstly very little ever goes wrong and secondly if he does need treatment he almost seems to know what is happening and becomes resigned to the fact that he needs an injection or has to be tubed with an ozogastric tube.

'He appears to me to be a very intelligent horse, sometimes looking at us mere humans as silly in what we are trying to achieve with him. He has an even temperament, never getting ratty even in the most difficult circumstances and he has always been a very good long-distance traveller. He takes everything in his stride and never becomes stressed by any outside influence, so that when he got to where he was going he was able to compete to his full potential.

'I have certainly some great memories of Podge, the more notable being when he went in to do the dressage at Los Angeles. I swear to God that he grew one hand in height as he walked into that stadium. When Mark was warming him up before he went into the official arena in front of the crowd, he was really showing off. In fact the horse is a real showman. He certainly knew when a big event was at stake; and when he was performing for the crowd he gave that little bit extra.

'Similarly, the performance in the dressage in Korea was, I believe, one of the best tests I have ever seen. Both horse and rider seemed to be in harmony, and it made the hairs on the back of your neck stand up. I believe Podge's intelligence was also reflected in his cross-country: he never used more energy than he had to. He seemed to know the size of the combination and the distance that he needed to exert in order to jump, and he was obviously enhanced by the superb rider on his back. To see both him and Mark in action cross-country was a sight to behold.

'Podge appears to rise to the occasion whatever the job, and in the past few months travelling around New Zealand he seems to be at home entertaining children and well-wishers alike. It really is as if he knows exactly what is going on. It has indeed been a pleasure to work with such a combination as Charisma and Mark.

ABOVE: Charisma showing his elegance in a near-perfect medium trot circle during the dressage test at Seoul, 1988. RIGHT: Foot perfect.

'A piece of cake!'...

... Podge made this difficult water complex in Seoul look so easy.

ABOVE: Just checking. Show jumping at Seoul, 1988. RIGHT: Podge's second Olympic gold medal was the sweetest victory of them all.

confident, and that made me confident. He performed a brilliant dressage test – one that, along with his test in Luhmühlen, must have ranked as his most outstanding. I felt, as did many others who were watching, that he deserved a better score than the 37.6 penalties awarded to him. It put us into the lead, but only two points ahead of the German rider, Claus Erhorn.

There was a lot of comment and criticism of the cross-country course at Wondang Ranch. As with any new course, on the first walk it always looks very difficult, but I must admit that we were pleasantly surprised, maybe even a little disappointed, that the fences did not look that difficult. What did worry us, however, was that we had a very serious endurance test to pass before arriving on the cross-country. The roads and tracks were very long, and in the heat the sand roads had baked like concrete, and we thought the horses would get jarred up and sore. The steeplechase had a substantial incline that had to be climbed three times on the figure-of-eight course, and, added to that, the cross-country course was over hilly ground which was going to take a lot out of the horses.

Although the endurance element was very significant, I felt that the cross-country course itself was of a standard that most could cope with it. However, because there were complaints about some of the obstacles, the Ground Jury asked Hugh Thomas, the course designer, to make a few alterations. We were at the first water complex when a very upset Hugh came along to demolish the fence and to lower it by three inches.

ABOVE: Warming up in the main arena, Seoul. BELOW: Helen Gilbert holds the Kiwi mascot aloft. With her are fellow grooms Alison Duthie (left) and Elaine Pickworth.

Podge, always so quick and nimble, wastes no time taking the long route through Chosun's Choice at Seoul.

Clarissa Strachan (international three-day event rider):

'My memories of his prodigious talent and enormous character are innumerable, but my final memory sums him up to me totally. After the tremendous build-up to the Seoul Olympic Games we waited up all night to see the cross-country on television. It was quite obvious that Charisma knew that he was there to make history; we saw him complete by far the best round of the day, making it all look so easy, and then have the cheek to show off quite deliberately how fresh he still was with a smug extended trot – good enough to score a "10" – as he pulled up!

'What a character, and what a horse. I am very glad and grateful to have known him.'

Personally, I didn't think that this would make any difference at all. The horses would either jump it or not. However, I was quite relieved when they took out the first element of the Wondang Walls at 27 and 28. In its original state it was a difficult jump, coming at the end of the course when you could reasonably expect the horses to be very tired. But once it was modified, it was little more than a Novice fence.

Hugh had built an excellent course on a somewhat limited site. The countryside in Korea is extremely mountainous, and nearly all the flat land is occupied by rice paddies – not ideal for a three-day event. The roads and tracks ran through the local villages, which was certainly unusual. You could look into the people's houses and see what they were having for breakfast, and trot alongside paddy fields watching them at work. The local village people must have wondered what on earth was going on. Wondang Ranch, the site of the cross-country, was quite close to the border where the trouble was, and there were guards posted in all the fields around the roads and tracks: though I can't imagine what they would have done if we'd been attacked.

Podge bolted round the steeplechase, with me pulling on him all the way, and we finished with 20 seconds to spare. I could hardly stop him even when we got to the end of the track; he just wanted to keep going. Once again, I was the last to go for the New Zealand team. Marges Knighton had gone first and had had three stops, the last of these at the Taxi Stand, Fence 30, where her horse had just ground to a halt, apparently out of sheer exhaustion. Andrew Bennie and Grayshott had had a fall at the 25th fence, but they had also arrived home safely and then Tinks Pottinger rode a great round with Volunteer to be the first to achieve a clear within the time. Her performance certainly put our team in contention, and it also confirmed that it was possible to make the time.

Even so, I decided to set off reasonably steady and to play it by ear. I didn't want to exhaust the horse, but if he felt all right I could increase the pace later on. I should have known better: Podge makes his own rules. He stormed out of the box like a demon, and all I could do was try to settle him and steady him a bit without having a fight over it. When we reached my first time-check point, at 4 minutes, he was already 15 seconds under, which amazed me. I knew we'd been going faster than I'd intended, but I didn't think we'd been going *that* fast. From there on I just let him cruise round at his own pace. He was never under pressure at any stage, and I never had to kick him. He finished the course

absolutely full of running, again with the fastest time of the day.

At the end of the cross-country course the horses had their recovery rates checked. The vets were amazed that Podge, at the age of sixteen, and having clocked the fastest time of the day, had one of the best recovery rates of all the horses. He had stopped blowing within ten minutes of finishing, which was incredible. And, again, the next day he came out as perky as ever, with no stiffness or other problems.

He knew that he was a star. Even at the vets' inspections he used to love showing off to the crowd. He'd stand around with his head up in the air, ears pricked, posing for the spectators; and when it came to his turn to go in front of the Ground Jury, he'd flash off at the trot with extravagant action, making sure that he'd been noticed. The spectators loved him, and he was always given a big hand.

Our fast cross-country round meant that we maintained our lead position, and in fact had two fences in hand. Ginny Leng was lying second with Master Craftsman, and very close to her was Ian Stark with Sir Wattie. As far as the team scores went, Germany seemed to be in an unassailable position, well clear of Britain and New Zealand, who were left to battle it out for the silver medal. Marges Knighton's Enterprise had been spun at the final vets' inspection, and when Andrew Bennie and Grayshott had five show jumps down it was clear that the team

Nearing home on the cross-country at Seoul.

83

Ginny Leng (Olympic bronze medallist, World and European Champion):

'Like so many famous horses, Podge was not your typical three-day event horse. Small, chunky and in some ways pretty, Podge was not ideally suited to a 6ft 4in lean Mark Todd.

'Together they have made history. Podge snubbed the critics by winning a second individual medal at an age when most event horses would have been retired. To my mind, Mark and Podge won their second medal in one of the most classical performances I have ever watched. I feel very fortunate to have known them both.'

bronze was all we could hope for. Even so, that was the best result that had ever been gained by a New Zealand three-day event team at the Olympic Games, and we could be well pleased.

I wasn't too worried about the show jumping: the going suited Podge (it was hard sand, like Los Angeles) and although he was quite capable of having two rails down, I just felt that he knew this was a big occasion and that he wouldn't let me down.

Ginny Leng surprised us all by dropping two rails with Master Craftsman, which gave Ian Stark the silver medal and Ginny the bronze, and also left me with three fences in hand. That made me feel even more confident that we could win, and so I was able to be a little bit more relaxed when we went into the arena. Charisma was a nerve-racking horse to show jump at the best of times, because whenever you went over a fence you could hear this tap-tap as he touched the rails. I had got used to it, but it always made the crowds gasp anxiously, and I was often tempted to look round behind me to check that the rail hadn't come down.

The first half of the course went well. Then he knocked down the last

OPPOSITE: Seoul, 1988. Podge got me into the nervous habit of looking back at the fence when show jumping.

LEFT: Kiwi supporters.

fence coming out of the combination. We still had two rails in hand, and he continued to jump clear round the course, until we had just three fences left. Then I knew we had won. The third last was a triple bar, which he would never knock down, and although the last two fences were another combination it didn't matter if he had them both down. He jumped them all clear anyway.

This was the sweetest victory for me. We had defeated all the odds to come back and win two Olympic Games in succession. Charisma had proved wrong all the cynics who had said that he was too old and past his best. At sixteen years of age he had never been better, and I knew that he deserved this chance to defend his Olympic title. He had won his last competition in England, the British Open Championships at Gatcombe, and now he had won his last three-day event – the Olympics. It was just such a perfect way for him to end his career.

Back to back, facing the press.

7 The Best Horse in the World
by Helen Gilbert

My first impression of Charisma was that of a very small, overweight horse with a sun-bleached neck. Mark was standing next to him and I found it difficult to visualise the two of them competing together. I had come out to New Zealand to work for Mark in August 1983, mainly through being in the right place at the right time.

Mark and Charisma had already made their impression on New Zealand eventing by winning the national one- and three-day events shortly before I arrived, and once Podge came back in to work he very quickly became my favourite horse on the yard. He has always been a real character, letting everyone know that he was the most important person around.

He is a lovely horse to handle. You can do almost anything to him without him batting an eyelid, and he revels in as much attention as he can possibly get. Being stabled was quite new to him when Mark first got him, but he loved it. I'm sure he thought it was a bit of one-up-manship on the others left out in the paddock.

Podge has always enjoyed going to 'parties' (shows and events), and would get very cross and sulky when left behind. He has been known, on occasion, to get bored at events, detach himself from the horsebox and go for a walk on his own. I even remember that at one show he found he could pull one back shoe off by standing on the edge of it with the other foot. He did this three times in one day and was very unpopular!

He handled his first flight to England as though he'd been doing it all his life. I had gone to England a week before Mark and the horses, to get

---

Helen came to groom for me in New Zealand at the end of the 1983 season and she looked after Podge and my other horses until after the Seoul Olympics. Podge is one of those horses who has a lovely personality and, as with some humans, you can't help but like him. Helen became very attached to him, which meant that he was never short of attention and always had the best possible care. Initially I carried out most of the ridden work with Podge, but as I acquired more horses and as our team grew I did less and less. Helen used to do all the road work, and when we were away in New Zealand at the beginning of the year she would bring Podge up from his winter holiday and start his fittening programme. I still liked to do most of his canter work, and I always did his schooling.

Over the five years during which I had Podge there were very few people other than Helen and me who rode him. Helen always looked after him at competitions and made all the travel arrangements. Her help was invaluable, and I was incredibly lucky to have such a good groom.   M.T.

the yard and cottage organised, and then I went to the airport with Mimi May to collect them. It was a freezing cold February morning: a real shock for the arriving party, who had come from late summer in New Zealand. Poor Night Life, the other horse Mark took to England, had picked up a virus on the plane and was quite ill for a few days, but Podge was in great form and seemingly unaffected by the whole thing. He settled into his new surroundings really well. As long as he had food, warmth and lots of attention he was happy.

Once Podge had had a couple of weeks to get over the flight and to acclimatise we started his preparation for Badminton. He had been reasonably fit when he left New Zealand so now we just had to do the big build up for a three-day event. All the slow fittening work had to be done on the roads, as there was nowhere else to ride in the area (we were based at Charlie Cottenham's yard at Kington St Michael, near Chippenham), and with no decent slopes locally we had to travel by trailer to hills about half an hour away, two or three times a week.

Mark and Podge had a few problems in the lead-up events before Badminton but had a good run at Brigstock, which restored Mark's faith in the horse. Podge had no health or fitness problems in his preparation, and arrived at Badminton in excellent form. He trotted up at the first vets' inspection with his lovely free action, and passed. It's always a nerve-racking occasion, even when you know your horse is 100%.

He settled into his new stable really well, although he didn't care too much for the bars across his door. I just put a rope across his doorway all day so that he could look out and talk to anyone who went by. As he was in a strange stable I bandaged him at night, something we always do when we go away. It cuts down on the risk of injury in unknown surroundings.

The dressage went without problems, but on cross-country day I had

Georgina Cottenham sits proudly on her very chunky 'first pony' (alias Charisma).

Podge saddled up and ready ten minutes before they were due to start on Phase A and there was no sign of Mark. I took the horse up to the start box. Still no Mark. People were asking where he was. I shrugged them off, saying: 'He'll be here in time,' but inwardly getting a bit worried. I tightened the girths and noseband. Still no sign of him. Then he appeared in a flat-out run, leaped on to Podge and went through the start as they were counting him down – a bit too close for comfort. Mark told me later that he had gone back to his caravan to work out his cross-country times and had fallen asleep!

They sailed through the first three phases and came into the ten-minute box in great form. I checked all the shoes, studs, boots, etc., washed the horse down and kept him moving. Then it was time for them to set off on the cross-country and all I could do was squeeze into the TV tent, watch and pray.

Podge took the course in his stride and finished really well. Once Mark had weighed-in I was able to walk Podge back to the stables, wash him off, rug him and walk him until his breathing returned to normal. After that I applied cold kaolin to his legs, bandaged them, rugged him up and took him out to graze for as long as it was warm enough. I'm sure this helps to settle the horses mentally better than if they were put back into their stables.

We trotted him up at about 6pm and he seemed fine, so I left him in peace except for checking him before going to bed. He passed the second vets' inspection with no worries, and later that day jumped a lovely clear round to finish second. We were thrilled with him and the way in which he had coped with the 'big time'. Now we really were 'going for Gold'.

At this stage Podge had started to get a nasal discharge. We discovered from a series of tests and X-rays that this was coming from

---

Sarah Cottenham (event rider):

'When Podge first came to England, before the Los Angeles Olympics, he stayed with us at Kington St Michael. He soon acquired another name – "Georgina's first pony" – as our three-year-old daughter was privileged enough to have her first few rides on him. Photographs show a rather rotund pony only weeks away from becoming a leaner gold medal winner.

'During his two years with us he lived in a wonderfully carefree atmosphere. Unlike most of the top British three-day event horses he was never wrapped in the proverbial cotton wool. He hardly saw any boots or bandages, and, because he was everyone's friend, he could be safely turned out in a field with four other horses – all with shoes on – which actually happened just five days before travelling to Los Angeles.

'Only a thoroughly level-headed pony like Podge could have adapted so easily to the very varied situations in which he found himself. At the celebratory party we gave for him and Mark after Los Angeles he made his appearance late on in the evening. He didn't bat an eyelid when he poked his head round the front door amid the raucous and inebriated jollification of seventy of his keenest fans. He took it all in his stride and calmly bade goodnight by leaving his mark on the threshold. It was so placed as if to say: "I too can make difficult obstacles for you to negotiate."'

his sinuses and could only think that it was his reaction to the virus that Night Life had contracted on the flight from New Zealand. He was put on a course of tablets which seemed to help for a while, but these couldn't be given to him before or during a three-day event. Later on we used a Cromovet inhaler which worked very well. This was used as a four-day course, once a month throughout the event season.

His fitness preparation for the Games was much the same as for Badminton, although because of his sinus condition I would try and find a hill to trot up each day, which helped clear his nose. He was still on a fairly strict diet, as we were always battling with the fat that had built up over several years.

About ten days before leaving for Los Angeles, a lump appeared below Podge's near hind hock. We think that he and Night Life had been fooling around in the paddock and Podge had got himself kicked. He wasn't lame, but it was a worry so close to a big event. I stood him in the whirlpool boot for as long as possible each day, and by the time Wally Niederer, the New Zealand's team vet, arrived it was a lot better, and very soon it had disappeared.

Several days before leaving, I cut Podge's feed so that he wasn't getting much protein during the long flight. All the trunks were packed and I just hoped that I hadn't left anything behind.

Podge seemed to enjoy the flight to Los Angeles, despite the delays. On arrival in Santa Anita the horses had to do 36 hours quarantine, which he hated. I'm sure he felt claustrophobic, as he was really miserable, but once he was outside it was a different story: he bucked all the way back to the New Zealand barn.

The barn was at the highest spot at Santa Anita, so if there was a slight breeze we had the benefit of it. The grooms' accommodation was directly above the horses, which was great for keeping an eye on things. Unfortunately there was no real grass at Santa Anita. The race-track was covered with a very thick, coarse grass that didn't appeal much to the horses, but at least it gave them a chance for a pick and a good roll.

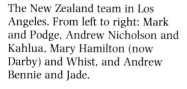

The New Zealand team in Los Angeles. From left to right: Mark and Podge, Andrew Nicholson and Kahlua, Mary Hamilton (now Darby) and Whist, and Andrew Bennie and Jade.

Podge acclimatised really well, and after a couple of days I had him back on his normal feed and Mark was working him hard.

Once again the vets' inspection was no problem, and in the dressage Podge really rose to the occasion: although when Mark asked for an extended trot before going into the arena the crowd gave him a standing ovation, and he went beserk. My heart sank, but in they went and did a lovely test, finishing in fourth place.

Almost immediately after the dressage we had to travel down to Fairbanks Ranch in San Diego for the cross-country. This meant that we had to pack and load everything before the dressage. Podge then had to be dope-tested, so once we were back in barn it was a real rush. The journey took over two hours and it was almost dark when we reached Fairbanks, so only the necessary gear was unpacked. The grooms' accommodation was in converted stables in between the horses. I had Podge's stable next to my bed and he spent the whole night digging up his dirt floor. The following morning I removed more boulders from his stable than manure!

The day was a rest day and it gave the horses a chance to get used to a different climate – a dry heat as opposed to the humidity of Santa Anita. The heat factor was a big worry on the cross-country, but we were able to wash the horses down after the steeplechase, and once they were in the ten-minute box we kept ice on the pulse points to cool them down and to help reduce the heart rates. We also washed them, checked all the gear, and of course kept them moving.

Again, Podge made nothing of the course and finished brilliantly. After Mark had weighed-in I cooled Podge down by washing him every five minutes or so and keeping him walking. He recovered very quickly and trotted up that evening sound and not at all stiff.

The next morning Mark thought we ought to lunge Podge as he might be stiff. We let the rope out and he tore off, bucking, turned around and came back doing a beautifully free, extended trot. 'Put him away,' said Mark. 'He's fine!'

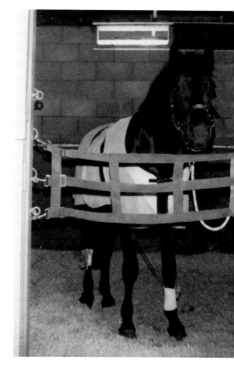

As a precautionary measure before the competition in Los Angeles, Podge wore an Ionacare machine to help ease a kick on his hind leg and a slight filling on a foreleg.

Podge arriving back at Santa Anita after the cross-country.

We headed back to Santa Anita as soon as the vets' inspection was over, so all the packing and loading had to be done early. The poor horses must have wondered what was going on. Once back at Santa Anita there was another rest day and I tried not to think that we were now in the silver medal place.

On show jumping day, Mark told me at what time I was to bring Podge down to the practice arena. I set off at the said time, only to be met by Andrew Bennie, telling me to wait another twenty minutes. This I did, and set off again, to be met this time by Andrew Nicholson who turned us back once more. We finally made it at the third attempt, and Mark started working in Podge with the help of Ted Edgar.

By now the butterflies were doing somersaults in my stomach, and when Mark and Podge went into the arena I was a nervous wreck. Podge managed, in his own style, to jump a clear round, and as he jumped the last, Ted Edgar threw me into the air. I couldn't believe it. A silver medal!

Podge came out of the arena looking really pleased with himself. Mark jumped off and went back to watch Karen Stives, and I took Podge out to the practice arena to wait. Complete silence had descended on the stadium as the American jumped her round, but suddenly the crowd gasped and I realised that she must have knocked a fence down. I burst into tears, and the next thing I knew was that everyone was congratulating us. Eventually we found Mark in the crowds. He was still in a state of shock.

Podge knew what he had done. During the medal ceremony, at the precise moment when the medal was put over Mark's head, Podge nipped me on the arm as if to say: 'We did that.' I was reduced to tears again.

Podge then had to have another dope test, as did all the medal winners. He duly obliged, and then it was celebration time. He joined in the party and even had some Champagne.

The next morning I received a horrible shock when I was mucking out Podge's stable and I dug up a riding boot. Luckily there was no leg attached to it. It was one of Mark's – ripped off him along with almost all his clothes the night before. I also found his shirt in the stable.

Podge was really tired that day: more so than I've ever seen him before or since, and I'm sure it was because the event went on for a lot longer than normal, and mentally it had worn him out. He wasn't even interested in going down to the track for a pick of grass and a roll; he kept pulling back and trying to turn round. Once at the track he had a quick roll and marched off back towards the barn looking very determined. That evening we went for another short walk, but otherwise I just left him in peace.

The next day was a different story, he was leaping around like a lunatic on the end of the rope. So after that I rode him each day. That was typical of him though: he always bounced back.

We had almost another week at Santa Anita before flying back to England. I hacked Podge around the complex each day just to keep him ticking over, and cut his feed to prepare for the journey home. Once back in England he was turned out on holiday, something he eventually got used to, although he would rush up and greet anyone who went past the field and demand attention from them.

*　　*　　*　　*

Podge had another uneventful preparation for Badminton in 1985 and seemed in greater form than ever. He was now really beginning to be a little ball of muscle with virtually all of the 'old fat' gone. He *almost* won Badminton: but then that's so often been the story. Instead, he came second again. It's terrible to think that a year before, we had been thrilled at him coming second, and this time we were disappointed.

That same year we had two changes of yards and ended up at Cholderton House. It's a beautiful yard with marvellous facilities, and as it is on the edge of Salisbury Plain we had endless miles of tracks and grass to ride on, also some good hills, so the fitness work was a lot easier. Podge came up really well in the spring of '86 and began his preparation for the World Championships in Australia. We were still having to use the Cromovet inhaler, but apart from the discharge from his sinuses there were no other problems.

The horses had to be in quarantine before leaving for Australia and we joined the English, German and Irish teams at Wylye in Wiltshire. Wylye is the most tremendous preparation area for event horses, so we had no problems with their fitness training, and Podge felt wonderful.

During quarantine we had the chance to get the horses used to Australian feed and hay. The hay was flown over at great expense, and most horses thought it was awful – it was just like straw – but Podge tucked into it as though there were no tomorrow.

A week before we were to leave for Australia, a one-day event was organised within quarantine to give the horses a competitive run which they hadn't had for several weeks. Podge was very full of himself and was virtually out of control during the first half of the cross-country. Apparently he stood way off a palisade fence and hit it very hard with his off-hind stifle. He finished the course very lame, and by the time I got him back to the stables he could hardly put the injured leg on the floor.

Mark had to rush off, as Badminton was starting that day, so I was left to tend to Podge. That night I fomented the area, which was swelling up to the size of a football, to try and ease the pain and help the bruising. He was slightly happier the next day, although reluctant to put any weight on the leg. Luckily Ann Scott-Dunn was at Wylye with a laser machine, so she got to work on him, and within a couple of days the swelling was going and he was virtually sound again.

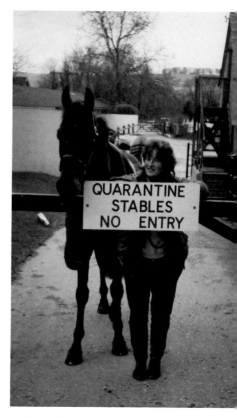

Podge and me, waiting to be let out of quarantine at Wylye, before our departure to Gawler, Australia.

Lizzie Purbrick (international event rider):

'Charisma was a tremendous character. He was such fun, but Mark didn't always find his antics amusing, especially when it came to show jumping. I remember they had some terrific battles at Cholderton, and they would both come out of the indoor school steaming with rage, but each convinced that they had got the better of the other. The trouble was, they were both so strong-willed that neither would give in. If Charisma jumped badly at an event, it was usually because he and Mark had had a fight in the practice arena, and then Charisma would knock some jumps down in the arena, out of spite. He was such an intelligent horse; he used to treat the whole thing as a game, which was infuriating for Mark. Yet he always seemed to know when he'd gone too far, and he could sense when an occasion was important enough to warrant good behaviour. When he wanted to, Charisma could show jump brilliantly.'

By the time we left for Australia the swelling was moving down his leg, and when we got there after travelling for 36 hours his leg, from the hoof to the hock, was enormous. This didn't stop him from bucking and being an idiot as soon as his feet touched the tarmac at Adelaide Airport. I'm sure he was doing it just for the TV cameras!

Once we arrived at the quarantine station at Torrens Island (we still had another ten days to go), I walked Podge for about two hours, which got rid of most of the swelling. For the next couple of days I just quietly hacked him, slowly building up his feed. He was loving his new Aussie feed, whereas a number of horses were refusing to eat it – which was a worry.

Torrens Island was never intended to be a quarantine area for competing horses – so the training facilities were less than we had hoped for. The organisers had gone to a lot of trouble, and had ploughed a sand track for hacking on, but unfortunately this was so deep we couldn't use it much. At the other end of the scale, the cantering track was very hard, and although this did improve considerably it was difficult doing fitness work in such a limited area. The horses became rather bored with trotting round and round in circles for over an hour.

From quarantine we moved to Roseworthy Agriculture College, and by this stage Podge was completely recovered and Mark was working him hard again. It was much easier to keep up the fitness work, as there were miles of roads and tracks to explore and somewhere different to go each day.

We had to travel to the competition daily from the college, which was a bit of a nuisance, especially on cross-country day when, instead of grooming Podge after his round and putting him away, we had to wait for transport. It also meant that I couldn't afford to leave anything behind.

Dressage day, and Podge was working in brilliantly. They went into the arena and he all but blew up. I couldn't believe it. He was being horrible and came out looking really pleased with himself. I took him back to the stables, washed him down and put him away, I was furious with him and hardly paid him any attention for the rest of the day. That night when I went to check him before going to bed he came up and put his head against me for a cuddle, as if to say: 'Sorry, Mum.' I had to forgive him then.

The fall at the water jump on the cross-country was so unlucky, but that's eventing. Podge pulled up well, totally unaffected, and nearly got away from me when he saw some sheep being moved on a distant hill and became very excited.

Once again he trotted up at the second vets' inspection as free as ever. He had a couple of show jumps down and finished tenth. Some people were now saying that he was over the hill – all because of one fall. Eight weeks later he showed them that he wasn't when he went brilliantly at the Luhmühlen Three-Day Event in Germany and easily won the competition.

He had travelled back from Australia really well, although this time we were in transit for 48 hours and, coming into Luton, England, the pilot misjudged the landing and 'dropped' the plane 50ft on to the runway. There wasn't a horse or human left standing, but luckily there were only a few minor injuries – mainly grazes and bruising.

When we arrived home, Podge was as bright and cheerful as usual, and he couldn't understand why I left him out in the paddock that

OPPOSITE: This photo says it all – the sheer pleasure and harmony of a brilliant duo. Los Angeles, 1984.

ABOVE LEFT: Podge pulling a face for the camera. ABOVE: Podge and me about to give a display during his victory tour of New Zealand after the Seoul Olympics. LEFT: Podge with Pam Bailey at his retirement home at Tirau in the North Island.

night. The weather was lovely and Mark thought that it would be better for Podge to stay out and keep moving after such a long confinement, but *he* didn't have to listen to Podge screaming to come in all night!

Badminton 1987 was cancelled at the last minute. We were about to start loading the horses on to the truck when the call came, so I had to turn around and unpack everything. We then hacked the horses, who couldn't understand what was going on. Podge was meant to win that year, too. He was looking and going better than ever. Instead he went to France and won the Saumur three-day event. Not quite Badminton, but never mind.

A lot of New Zealanders had booked to go and watch Badminton that year, and when it was cancelled they came in a steady stream to Cholderton to look around the yard and see the horses. Podge loved all the adoration – although he would eventually get bored with his public and turn his back on them. When one couple came in to see him he had already lost interest, so they went to take photos of the yard. Podge, who normally won't go out of his stable unless told, shot out through the open door, cantered straight up to the couple and literally 'posed' in front of them, as if to say: 'You can take my photo now'.

Later that year he came so close to winning Burghley when Mark did a first and second with Wilton Fair and Podge. I think a lot of people had hoped that it would be the other way around. I know I did, but Wilton was the better horse on the day.

In 1988 Podge had a really quiet spring. Mark wanted to just keep him ticking over: which was easier said than done. He came in that January like a four-year old. He was naughtier than ever out hacking, and I'm sure he couldn't understand why he didn't do a three-day event in the spring as in every other year. He would sulk when the horsebox went out without him and refuse to talk to us when we got home. He was normally the one happy face you could guarantee seeing when coming into the yard.

He worked really well in his build up to Seoul, and I believe that he was physically better than he had ever been in his life. He was beside himself when he went to his first one-day event in four months. Holker Hall was the final trial for the British team, and although the New

Major Malcolm Wallace (Director General of the British Equestrian Federation):

'My rather special recollection of Charisma was at the Nations Cup meeting at Hickstead in 1988. I was asked by the organising committee whether the crowd would appreciate seeing the combination. Mindful of the limitations that most three-day event horses have in the dressage department, and mindful also of the crowd that had come to watch show jumping, I rather advised them against it. How wrong I was. In the brilliant sunshine of the Hickstead arena, Mark and Charisma absolutely captivated the crowd. Looking even taller than normal in top hat and tails, Todd conjured up a most brilliant dressage display in and out of the gigantic fences and in the shadow of the Derby Bank. With some very advanced movements, the little horse literally danced around the arena with an elegance and charm with which most Grand Prix competitors would be delighted. As a combination, they drew more applause than the winners of the Nations Cup!'

Intelligence written all over his face. Charisma in quarantine at Cholderton before setting off for Seoul.

Zealand squad had already been selected, Podge went so badly that he nearly blew his chances of going to Seoul. He just couldn't contain himself the whole weekend, and he was even really naughty to handle; something he never normally is.

The following weekend he won the British Open Championship at Gatcombe. He behaved beautifully the whole time and it was a great way for him to finish his career in England. It also gave his critics something to think about for Seoul. I had won the turnout prize at Gatcombe with him, and as this was my last event in England grooming for Mark it was a good way for me to go as well.

We had to be in quarantine before Seoul, and the bottom yard at Cholderton had been passed by the authorities for us to use. We had seven horses from our yard in quarantine: Mark's three, Tinks Pottinger's two, and two from Santé de La Roche (Spain). Quarantine at home made life a lot easier, and I was still able to keep an eye on the top yard and help out when possible.

Podge was really happy in his new stable, although he couldn't understand why no one was allowed to visit him. It was quite difficult keeping the quarantine horses away from the others, especially out hacking. There were often great cries of 'don't come any closer!'

We were taking all our feed out from England to Seoul, which lessened any difficulties in that area. The water could have been a problem. The British took a water purifier and the French had bottled mineral for Jappaloup, but the tough Kiwi horses drank the Korean water and suffered no ill effects at all, which is more than I can say for some humans who sampled it.

Podge had thoroughly enjoyed his flight to Seoul. Lufthansa had allocated him a double space on the plane instead of the normal one-and-a-half spaces, because he was the Olympic Champion. I told them he would be fine with one-and-a-half spaces – he was after all the smallest horse on the flight – but they wouldn't have it, and he travelled in style.

Once off the plane, the horses' feet were sprayed and then we headed for Kwa'Chon Equestrian Park. As in Los Angeles, the horses had to do 36 hours quarantine, and then it was on to the New Zealand barn. Podge had a couple of small mascots who sat on a ledge in his stable and he would amuse himself for hours throwing them around his stable and trying to drown them in his water bucket.

After a couple of days' rest the horses were back in full work and Podge, having decided that this was serious stuff, hardly put a foot wrong. As at Los Angeles, there was very little edible grass for the horses, but at least they got a chance for a pick each day. A couple of tracks had been carved out of the hillside for us to use as hacks, which was useful, but we were constantly under the watchful eye of the South Korean guards – which was slightly unnerving.

Podge was a star in the dressage, rising to the occasion with the test of his life. We then had to go for a random dope test, as in Los Angeles, and then rushed back in time to leave for the cross-country site.

The New Zealand block of stables at Wondang Ranch was very temporary and had soft dirt floors. Podge, as in Los Angeles (it was almost a mirror event), soon discovered this, and within about ten minutes had dug a two-foot deep crater. The Koreans couldn't understand why I needed more bedding until I showed them the hole. They thought the whole thing hilarious.

Cross-country day, and Podge was raring to go. I took him for a walk early on and he was really full of himself. Eventually it was time for Mark to start. I saw them off on Phase A, met him at the start of the steeplechase – everything was fine. I then set off to the free zone at the end of the steeplechase, laden down with all the spare gear, trying to watch Mark and Podge at the same time. Podge pulled up really well and Mark was so far delighted with him. I washed the horse to help him cool down, squeezed a sponge out in his mouth and they set off again.

They came into the ten-minute box looking good, and I set about loosening gear, checking boots, shoes, studs, etc. We cooled Podge with ice, washed him down, and kept him moving. Very soon it was time to grease his legs, tighten up everything, and they were off. I rushed towards the nearest TV monitor. Podge seemed to be in his element. He loved every minute, and when he pulled up he looked as though he could have gone round again.

Once Mark had weighed in I took Podge to a vet who checked the heart rates, washed the horses down and checked the hearts again after five minutes to make sure the recovery rates were satisfactory. The vet

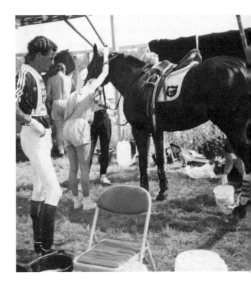

Mark looking pensive while Podge is attended to in the ten-minute box at Seoul.

Karen Lende (member of the US three-day event team, Seoul):

'I vividly remember watching Mark Todd's and Charisma's ride with all the riders who could squeeze into the tent to watch the closed circuit TV. They were remarkable. Mark had plenty of horse left at the end – twenty seconds inside the time. When he crossed the finish, the cheers nearly blew the tent down. There was cheering, screaming, hooting, clapping, and even some tears. It was a fairy tale coming true that we probably won't witness again in our lifetimes.'

ABOVE LEFT: Podge and I share a moment of sheer joy on winning the Los Angeles gold medal. ABOVE RIGHT: A similar picture, taken at the end of the Seoul Olympics, this time showing my utter relief that my beloved horse had won.

told me that Podge had one of the best heart rates to finish, and when she took it the second time said that it was the best recovery rate all day. Not bad for a sixteen-year-old!

Once back at the stables, I put ice packs on Podge's legs, washed him and walked him as I had done in Los Angeles. After about an hour I changed the ice for cold kaolin poultice and found some grass for him to pick at. When we trotted him up that evening you wouldn't have known he'd done a thing. The same applied when he trotted up for the vets' inspection the next day. He hadn't stiffened up at all; he had his ears pricked and wore an expression that could have said: 'That was easy. When does it get tough?'

I don't think I have ever felt as ill as I did on the day of the show jumping. Everyone was telling me not to worry, as Podge had so many fences in hand, but I knew that he could easily knock plenty down if he felt like it. They went into the arena. I had everything possible crossed, and I just prayed. I was holding on to someone's arms throughout the round and they showed me the bruises the next day!

It was the longest round ever, and I couldn't believe it when they came out winners. It was a fairy tale come true. Podge had really put his name in the history books now, and what a way to go into retirement. I had also decided that after being with Mark for five years it was time for me to 'retire', too, and move on. What a way to go.

*   *   *   *

I stayed on with the New Zealand and Aussie horses for the further quarantine, and of course I wanted to take Podge home. Life at Kwa'Chon after the Olympics was far from easy. The Koreans had lost

100

interest and made things very difficult. We were therefore thrilled when we finally left for Australia four weeks later.

Our stop-over in Melbourne was much better, and there was even a paddock to turn the horses out in: something we hadn't been able to do for over two months. The horses loved their freedom and spent hours playing games with each other (they were turned out in pairs). Podge found that just below the top soil was a thick layer of chalk. It was too good to resist, and he dug a larger hole each day, having wonderful rolls in it and coming out grey. By this time the horses that had come from the Northern Hemisphere had grown winter coats, and Podge was looking like a little black teddy bear.

Once back in New Zealand, a victory tour had been organised, and I was asked to take Podge round the country. The tour lasted for six months, and in that time we extensively covered both the North and South Islands. I would think that about three-quarters of New Zealand's population came to see their national hero, and he was amazing.

He had to stand for hours on end in a pen with his 'public' all trying to pat him. Mostly he was inside one of the many Wrightsons stores around the country (Wrightsons had sponsored the tour). Quite often

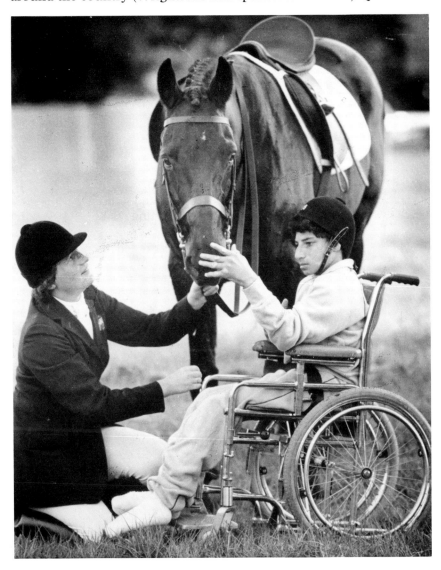

There surely cannot be a kinder horse. Here Podge makes friends with a disabled admirer.

> **Tiny Clapham (international event rider):**
>
> 'All the best things come in little parcels, and Charisma is definitely one of them. I feel privileged to have seen the partnership competing over the last five years. We'll never see another one like it.'

he would have to go through the front door of the shop then up a flight of steps and walk on carpets. All this he took in his stride. We also went to numerous shows, race meetings, trotting clubs and schools, and he visited several old peoples' homes. The reception everywhere was stupendous. People would get very emotional at the thought of touching him, and he was marvellous with disabled people, always giving them more time than others.

The tour certainly tested his temperament to the full. He was on show an average of five days a week and we covered approximately 28,000 kilometres (17,399 miles). He came through it all still with a smile on his face, loving people and demanding more attention. He showed what he is – a true champion and national hero – and he lived up to his name, Charisma.

Now that it is all over he is still being worked. He hates holidays. He's as sound as a bell and has hardly any blemishes. Provided he keeps getting plenty of cuddles and attention from those who love him he will stay a very happy horse.

I feel incredibly proud to have been involved with Mark and Charisma for such a long time. The Olympic Games were definitely the highlights, and I think Seoul would have the edge over Los Angeles. It was just a bit more special.

A journalist asked me once how I would describe Podge in one sentence. 'That's easy,' I said, 'his name says it all.' He just oozes Charisma.

BELOW LEFT: Advertisement for Charisma's victory tour. BELOW RIGHT: Fan mail.

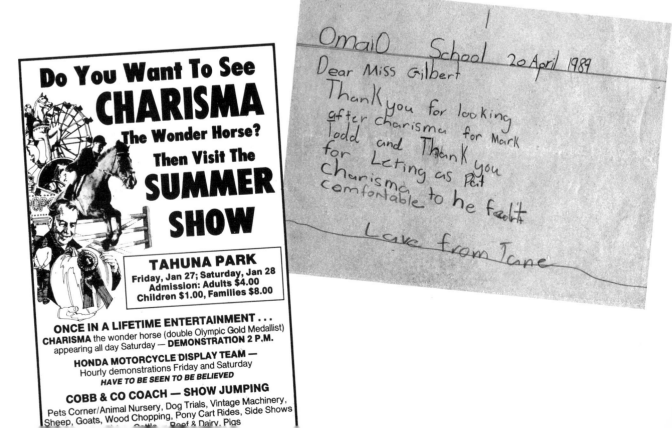

8 New Zealand's Pride
by Joan Gilchrist

Editor, New Zealand Horse and Pony

I'd love to be able to say that I had recognised the potential champion the moment I laid eyes on him . . . but it would be a lie if I did. I was, however, conscious that it wasn't often that one saw the quality of dressage at Pony Club and Novice level eventing – especially in New Zealand in 1981 – that Charisma produced the first time I recall seeing him.

It was at the Wills One-Day Horse Trials Championships at the South Island venue of Otaio, near Timaru, followed a week later by the Wills Three-Day Event Championships at Ashburton. The one-day event was just a week after he and Sharon had been in the box seat for the top award at the Pony Club Championships, which they lost because of a shy at the finish flags in the show jumping.

They led the dressage for the Ferndale Trophy, the National Novice One-Day Championship, but picked up 11.2 time penalties across country which, despite a clear show jumping round, relegated them to fifth at the end of the day. But he was the kind of horse that one filed at the back of one's mind for future reference, with the reservation that he was, perhaps, a mite small for the big time.

The Three-Day Event Championships were held over the same course as that year's Pony Club team championships, with a few additions and alterations to increase its distance and severity. Again, the dressage was out of the ordinary, and Charisma and Sharon led the field for the Mamaku Trophy – appropriately enough presented for the Novice Championship by the Williams family, 'Podge's' breeders.

Sharon will not thank me for remembering that in those days her cross-country rounds were inclined to be somewhat noisy as she encouraged the horse at every fence – with 'hup, hup, hups' and 'down, down, downs' – which I recall, even at this distance in time, along with the fact that the horse was clearly very talented. Not that he appeared to be the least affected by the vocal accompaniment, making his own arrangements to clock a good clear round inside the time. A clear show jumping round ensured them of the title and the Mamaku Trophy, named after Charisma's birthplace.

The following year, 1982, the pair won the Canterbury Novice One-Day, upgrading for the open class at the province's Two-Day Trial where, despite 24.4 time penalties across country, they took the first prize.

That was after they had been to their fourth Pony Club Championships, with Sharon as captain of the Canterbury Westland team. They'd won the junior dressage trophy in 1980 and the senior the following year, when they'd been second for the overall senior championship.

Once again, at Auckland, they proved their superiority in dressage and were a pleasure to watch. Cross-country day turned out horribly wet and windy, and the ground conditions deteriorated rapidly, turning the course into a treacherous, dangerous trial for the youngsters. I saw Charisma only briefly as he passed where I was on duty as a mounted steward. Few were clear; far too high a proportion were eliminated, retired or fell; the pair got round, but with 104.80 penalties and at the counting up were nowhere, adding to their score with one rail down and time faults in the show jumping.

By 1983's Horse of the Year Show, Charisma was in the North Island, and Jennifer Stobart had him at Auckland for his new owner, Fran Clark, placing several times at Medium level and again attracting my attention, as I remarked in N.Z. *Horse & Pony*: on 'that most versatile and talented horse, Charisma'.

Somewhere between that event and the National One-Day Horse Trials Championship, Toddy had been introduced to Podge at the suggestion of Horse Trials Publicity Officer, Virginia Caro. It was an inspired suggestion. There wasn't much time to get the weight down and the condition on, but they did it, and with one win behind them,

Charisma with his breeders, Peter and Daphne Williams, at Mamaku Station in 1989.

Charisma and Mark started favourites for the national title.

My report says: 'Charisma . . . recorded a superb performance in the test for the Advanced horses, scoring 37.50 . . . His lateral movements were well ahead of any of the other entrants . . .' They were clear across country, but picked up 2.4 time penalties and a further 1.25 time faults show jumping, but it was good enough to win the coveted Forest Gate Trophy and to go to the National Three-Day Event a couple of weeks later firmly in the favourite's position and with thoughts of Olympic representation beginning to form more substantially in the minds of those with Los Angeles as a target.

The pair did, of course, complete the double, as I again commented in *Horse & Pony*: 'confirming beyond any shadow of a doubt his [Mark's] supremacy as an eventing rider'. On this occasion, the dressage score was 39.67, although I felt that the 'test lacked the fluency this combination has shown themselves capable of'. Well, they couldn't be perfect every time, could they! (As an aside, it's interesting that a few paragraphs later, I remarked: 'If there was one horse that caught most eyes over the weekend it was Tinks White's (Pottinger) Volunteer, a smart brown six-year-old with the stamp of a real eventer' . . . at least I recognised that champion in the embryo stages!)

The cross-country that year at the National Equestrian Centre at Taupo looked a bit different from anything we'd seen before in New Zealand, thanks to a couple of Canadians – Nick Holmes-Smith and Shaun Flynn – who'd revamped the track and introduced some very new fences. Charisma was last to go in the Advanced class, and the new, exciting pairing looked every inch champions for only 0.4 time faults to hold the lead, show jumping clear to clinch the title for the Wills Trophy.

That was in June. In December, they and the other Olympic hopefuls competed in a specially staged Olympic trial event under the eagle eye of then FEI eventing committee chairman, Vicomte Jurien de la Gravière. Charisma won the dressage by more than 15 points, cruised the cross-country again at Taupo and was clear show jumping with one time penalty to score his fifth straight win with Toddy. He did, however, demonstrate that nerve-racking (for spectators and rider) propensity to tap his way around the show jumping – 'jumping by Braille' one journalist said after his Los Angeles gold medal round.

Then, of course, Charisma left for Britain and we didn't meet again until Los Angeles and that first magic gold medal for New Zealand eventing.

Euphoria was followed by a hollow feeling when it seemed that Charisma would be lost to Toddy, either by way of an international sale or by being returned to New Zealand by his then owner who didn't seem to be able to make up her mind. Certainly, in the days following the medal win, there was an enormous amount of activity to ensure that the 'bionic pony' would still be around to wear the silver fern at Gawler two years on at the World Championships. That, of course, culminated in his sale to Bill Hall via Lizzie Purbrick, so that the partnership might continue its winning ways.

The centre of all the furore knew nothing of it, concentrating as is his wont on his own interests, particularly food! He knew, at that memorable stable party at Santa Anita, that he was the champ, as he looked over his box door at the antics of us silly humans. As one fan remarked: 'He has the eye of an eagle, flying high above, looking down at us all.'

Mark and Charisma emerging as an exciting prospect for New Zealand, at Taupo way back in 1983.

At Gawler two years later, he travelled back to the Southern Hemisphere with his usual aplomb – indeed Helen Gilbert has said 'he thinks aeroplanes were invented for him' – and, although falling in the water, once again demonstrated his talent and personality. After a ducking such as he took not many horses would have gone on to complete the course so well.

The next time I saw Podge was at Cholderton, Salisbury, in 1987 – the year Badminton was cancelled – and his last chance to win the big one. As I watched the Crown Prince of Cholderton, which he undoubtedly was, munch his hay, up to his knees in shredded newspaper (any other bedding was regarded as edible), I reflected that here was the best horse never to have won Badminton.

We said hello again, around the same time in 1988, when he was getting ready for the Olympics and I was again en route for Badminton. I've only met a couple of horses other than Charisma who actually looked interested in visitors. His superb temperament and being a 'people' horse must be a big part of his secret. Despite the doubts about taking a sixteen-year-old to Seoul, I couldn't help thinking as I looked at him in his box that he carried his years so lightly as to make such concern unnecessary.

He was his usual self at Seoul, reacting to the atmosphere, aware that this was no ordinary event. We all hoped and believed he was capable of the double gold; we knew his capacity to rise to the big occasion had to reinforce the belief. But how often, I kept asking myself, do such fairy stories come true other than in fiction? That double gold that the Kiwis had so narrowly missed at Gawler kept intruding as Podge and Toddy moved inimitably towards the ultimate success. It was hard not to hold one's breath, to feel that something or someone would dash all the hopes at the last minute. Not least were we concerned about the show jumping . . . would he, or would he not be in the mood? And that was a part of what the horse is. With most horses, we know whether it's a good, mediocre or poor show jumper and, for the most part, can predict a performance within a rail or two. Not so with Charisma. We knew it didn't depend on his ability. He had that. The gold medal or not depended on how he felt when he got out of bed that last morning – it could be a clear round or it could be five rails!

He'd always responded to atmosphere, to the size and buzz of an event. He came into the ring looking around at the crowd, the flags, the cameras, feeling the tension . . . and he'd obviously slept well and wakened in the mood that makes champions.

Afterwards, as the world's media crowded around Todd, I wrote: '. . . the other half of the combination was cocking his cheeky head and submitting with ill-disguised disgust to the hugs and kisses of these strange humans. You could not help feeling that he knew what it was all about – Todd and the horse's personal handmaiden, Helen Gilbert, were quite sure he was totally aware'.

At the stables that night Toddy, in shocking pink Bermudas and equally garish shirt, rode Charisma in his headcollar to the door of the barn to greet his fans . . . the Brits, for whom he was almost one of their own, the Americans, the Irish, the Canadians, the Australians . . . and the New Zealanders, some of us who had followed the little black power-pack through most of his career. As we cheered him, his big eyes sparkled, he acknowledged the toasts, the love, the admiration – and I doubt I was the only one with a tear in the eye. It was a poignant

A cutting from *The Sunday Times*.

SEOUL 88: A PLACE IN HIST

The odd couple who clinched it more than once

Dudley Doust reports on the triumph of New Zealand's Mark Todd and Charisma

THEY'RE an odd couple of poise and balance, he has suf-
vis, a mismatch at first fered a spectrum of injur-
he's gaunt, since he hashed acro

> **Pegotty Henriques (dressage writer for Horse and Hound):**
>
> 'Of all the classes that I watched in Seoul, one of the tests that gave me the greatest pleasure was Charisma's in the dressage phase of the three-day event.
>
> 'Mark Todd is a superlative horseman and Charisma is aptly named. The test they showed together was as good as you need to see at this level and probably more faultless than the Grand Prix Special that gold medallist Uphoff and Rembrandt performed.'

moment, because we knew we'd seen the last of this combination that had, over five years, provided so many marvellous eventing moments at home and internationally.

I was on the tarmac when Charisma came home, the November following Seoul. He came down the ramp from the flight crate, looked around with that bright eye, and claimed his territory. He also saw the television cameras and characteristically presented his best side! He is incorrigible, but it's not arrogance, it's the self-assuredness of a champion.

Home again. Mark and Carolyn reunited with Charisma on New Zealand soil. November 1988.

In the months after his return, he demonstrated another facet of that special character. With Helen Gilbert, he travelled New Zealand in a countrywide victory tour. It was to a hero's welcome everywhere, but it involved him in closest contact with his adoring public, so many of whom had no experience of horses, let alone a highly-tuned model like Charisma. It was a miracle he had any tail left, so many hairs were pulled. He was petted, patted, slapped, pushed, photographed and gawped at, and never once lost his cool or his patience. From tiny tot to adoring octogenarian, he tolerated their advances and approaches. Only once, in the tension after a very nerve-racking city-centre parade did he get upset, knocking down an old man who was much too close for comfort. It says an enormous amount for his temperament that by the end of that tour he was not thoroughly soured of all human contact.

In June 1989 he was back at Taupo's National Equestrian Centre, scene of his first three-day triumph with Mark. Helen brought him out on dressage morning and his expression indicated: 'Oh, dear, not another day on show?' But within a few minutes, his head was up; he looked as if he'd grown four inches; and the eye was saying 'Hey, this is a three-day event . . . O.K., I'm ready'! He was delighted to show off in the dressage arena on the first day. On endurance day he came out 17 hands high, three inches above the ground and 'ready for off'! No way was he interested in quietly walking around in a stewarding role . . . he was going jumping if somebody would just give him half a chance! Helen had an exciting day on him, and those watching closely might just have seen the Olympic champion hopping over a couple of small fences when he thought nobody was looking!

He has spun a spell over those who have known him. Like many of my colleagues in equestrian journalism, I have known good, even great horses . . . but of them all, Charisma has left some very special memories as well as some of the most exciting stories I've had to write.

Charisma with an admiring group of young fans at his homecoming.

APPENDIX I

Charisma's Competition Record

YEAR	EVENT	PLACE
IN NEW ZEALAND		
1979	*With Sharon Dearden*	
	Novice Dressage Championships	1st
	Junior Equitation Finals	1st
	NZ Pony Club Championships	4th (team)
1980	Canterbury Junior Dressage Trophy	1st
1981	NZ Pony Club Championships	2nd
	National Novice Three-Day Event	1st
	Open One-Day Event	1st
	Intermediate Two-Day Event	1st
1982	Canterbury Novice One-Day Event	1st
	Canterbury Two-Day Trial	1st
1983	*With Jennifer Stobart*	
	Dressage Horse of the Year Championship	4th
	With Mark Todd	
	One-Day Event (NZ) Southern Hawkes Bay	1st
	National One-Day Event Championships, Clevedon	1st
	National Three-Day Event, Taupo	1st
	One-Day Event Olympic Trial, Taupo	1st

YEAR	EVENT	PLACE
BASED IN ENGLAND		
1984	**One Day Events**	
March	Aldon	unplaced
"	Rushall	unplaced
"	Brigstock	unplaced
April	**Badminton** Three-Day Event	2nd
June	Tweseldown One-Day Event	4th
July	Castle Ashby One-Day Event	3rd
Sept/Oct	**Los Angeles Olympic Three-Day Event**	1st
1985	**One-Day Events**	
March	Crookham	1st
"	Aldon	1st
"	Brigstock	1st
April	**Badminton** Three-Day Event	2nd
	One-Day Events	
June	Heckfield	1st
July	Dauntsey	unplaced
Aug	Gatcombe British One-Day Open Championship	1st
Sept	Bourton	1st
Oct	Castle Abbey	1st
1986		
March	Aldon One-Day Event	1st
April/May	Reynella, Australia, International One-Day Event	1st
May	Gawler, Australia, World Championships	10th
July	Frome One-Day Event	2nd
Aug	Luhmühlen Three-Day Event	1st
"	Thirlestane Castle One-Day Event	2nd
1987		
March	Dynes Hall One-Day Event	4th
April	Saumur Three-Day Event	1st
June	Stockholm Three-Day Event	6th
Aug	Molland One-Day Event	unplaced
"	Rotherfield Park One-Day Event	1st
"	Gatcombe British One-Day Open Championship	unplaced
Sept	**Burghley** Three-Day Event	2nd
1988	**One-Day Events**	
April	Belton Park One-Day Event	2nd
"	Brockenhurst Park One-Day Event	3rd
Aug	Holker Hall One-Day Event	unplaced
"	Gatcombe British One-Day Open Championship	1st
Sept	**Seoul Olympic Three-Day Event**	1st

LOS ANGELES OLYMPICS 1984

RIDER AND NATION	HORSE	DRESSAGE	ROADS & TRACKS	STEEPLECHASE	CROSS-COUNTRY JUMP	TIME	SHOW JUMPING	TOTAL
1 Mark Todd (NZL)	Charisma	51.60	—	—	—	—	—	51.60
2 Karen Stives (USA)	Ben Arthur	49.20	—	—	—	—	5	54.20
3 Virginia Holgate (GBR)	Priceless	56.40	—	—	—	0.4	—	56.80

SEOUL OLYMPICS 1988

RIDER AND NATION	HORSE	DRESSAGE	ROADS & TRACKS	STEEPLECHASE	CROSS-COUNTRY JUMP	TIME	SHOW JUMPING	TOTAL
1 Mark Todd (NZL)	Charisma	37.6	—	—	—	—	—	37.60
2 Ian Stark (GBR)	Sir Wattie	50.0	—	—	—	2.8	—	52.80
3 Virginia Leng (GBR)	Master Craftsman	43.2	—	—	—	8.8	10.00	62.00

APPENDIX 2   Charisma's Conformation

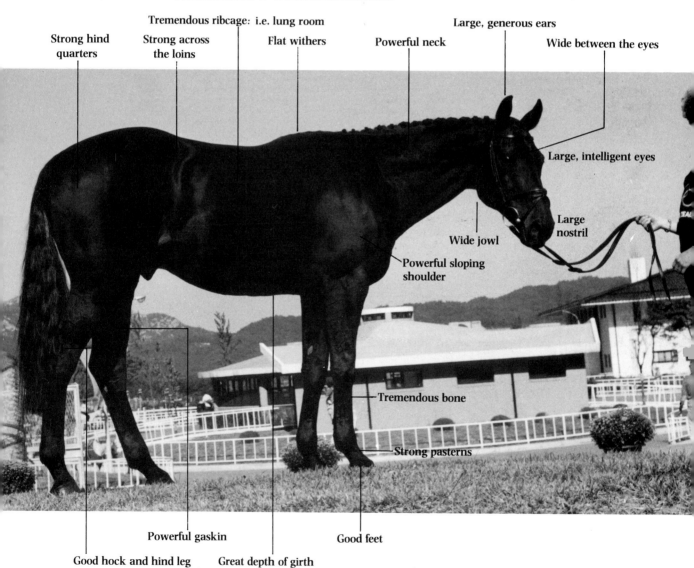

Strong hind quarters
Tremendous ribcage: i.e. lung room
Strong across the loins
Flat withers
Powerful neck
Large, generous ears
Wide between the eyes
Large, intelligent eyes
Large nostril
Wide jowl
Powerful sloping shoulder
Tremendous bone
Strong pasterns
Powerful gaskin
Good feet
Good hock and hind leg
Great depth of girth

INDEX

There are no index entries under Charisma nor his pet names, 'Stroppy' and 'Podge'. Similarly there are no index entries under Todd, Mark.

PICTURE CREDITS

E. Andersen, 60–1
Pam Bailey, 96 (bottom)
Alf Baker, 47 (top)
Barn Owl, 64 (both pictures)
Lady Cottenham, 88
Hugo Czerny, 36–7, 47 (bottom), 50 (left)
Sharon Dearden, 11, 17 (top left), 21 (centre), 105
S. Dickens, 14
Werner Ernst, 100 (left), 110
Leo Garennes, 63 (both pictures)
Helen Gilbert 9 (bottom), 28 (top), 29 (top), 79 (top), 90, 91 (both pictures), 93, 96
   (top right), 99 (top)
Joan Gilchrist, 8 (top left), 10, 21 (bottom), 96 (top left), 107
Gower Photos, 53
Kit Houghton, 21 (top right), 23, 27, 28 (bottom), 29 (bottom), 30, 33, 34 (both
   pictures), 40, 41, 43, 48–9, 50 (right), 51, 52, 62, 65 (both pictures), 66–7, 67,
   69 (both pictures), 70, 71, 73, 78 (all pictures), 79 (bottom), 80–81, 82, 84, 85
   (both pictures), 86, 97, 99 (bottom)
Bob Langrish, cover picture, 75 (both pictures), 76–77
Judith McEwen, 15, 22 (right)
New Zealand Herald, 100 (right), 101
Wally Niederer, 83, 98
Barbara Palmer, 9 (top right)
Mike Roberts, 8 (bottom right)
Elizabeth Purbrick, 45
Barbara Thomson, 17 (top right and bottom), 18 (both pictures), 22 (left), 57
   (bottom left and right), 109
Times-Age, 104, 108
Daphne and Peter Williams, 6, 7, 8 (top right and bottom left)
Wynyard Lodge Stud, 9 (top left)

In spite of having made every effort to trace the copyright owners of all the
photographs reproduced in this book, the publishers are aware that there were some
errors and omissions, and we would be grateful for any information regarding them.